D0944430

dogs
behaving
badly

RETIRÉ DE LA COLLECTION UNIVERSELLE

Bibliothèque et Archives nationales du Québec

Collins

gwen bailey

dogs
behaving
badly

a practical problem solver

First published in 2004 by
Collins, an imprint of
HarperCollins*Publishers*
77-85 Fulham Palace Road
Hammersmith
London W6 8JB

The Collins website address is www.collins.co.uk

Collins is a registered trademark of HarperCollins Publishers Ltd

10 09 08 07 06 05 04
7   6   5   4   3   2   1

© Text, Gwen Bailey, 2004
© Photographs and design, HarperCollins*Publishers,* 2004

Gwen Bailey hereby asserts her moral right to be identified as the author of this work.

All rights reserved. No part of this publication may be reproduced, stored in a retrieval system, or transmitted, in any form or by any means, electronic, mechanical, photocopying, recording or otherwise, without the prior written permission of the publishers.

Created by: SP Creative Design, Suffolk, UK
Editor: Heather Thomas
Design and production: Rolando Ugolini
Photography by Charlie Colmer and Rolando Ugolini

A catalogue record for this book is available from the British Library

ISBN 0 00 717492 6

Colour reproduction by Colourscan, Singapore
Printed and bound by L.E.G.O. SPA, Italy

Many of the dogs featured in this book were rehabilitated and rehomed by staff at the Danaher Animal Home for Essex. Care of dogs like these, who are still looking for new homes, is funded solely by voluntary donations so your donations and support would be greatly appreciated.

Danaher Animal Home for Essex
(A self-funded charity affiliated to the RSPCA – charity no. 1052282)
Headingham Road, Wethersfield, Essex EM7 4EQ

Contents

Introduction

All dog owners experience behaviour problems at some time during their dog's life. Whether these are major or minor, it is always useful to have a source of good advice to help deal with them quickly before they become a bad habit. This book will enable you to identify why your dog does what he does and will give you suggestions on how to resolve the problem.

It is always important to solve the problem for the dog rather than just treat the symptoms. Long-lasting cures involve finding out why your dog has a specific behaviour problem and trying to find a way for him to get

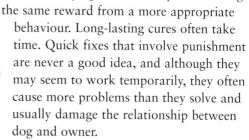

the same reward from a more appropriate behaviour. Long-lasting cures often take time. Quick fixes that involve punishment are never a good idea, and although they may seem to work temporarily, they often cause more problems than they solve and usually damage the relationship between dog and owner.

In order to include many subjects, space for each is limited, but each chapter covers every aspect of that type of problem to point you in the right direction. If you need further help, there are plenty of places to find it. Always start with your veterinary surgeon who can check that there is nothing physically wrong that may be causing the change in behaviour. Your veterinary practice should be able to refer you to an experienced pet behaviour counsellor if the problem is severe or if your dog is aggressive so that you can get first-hand help and advice. There is no shame in admitting you have a problem with your dog, however embarrassing the behaviour might be. Many owners will be facing similar problems. Most behaviour problems are natural, normal canine behaviours which are exhibited inappropriately for life with their humans, and usually they can be solved, particularly if they are minor. This book will help to start you off.

Note: Throughout this book, 'he' is written in preference to 'he/she'. Male dogs are slightly more prone to developing behaviour problems than females. The ratio of male to female dogs attending behaviour clinics is 6:4.

▶ Gwen Bailey with her dog Spider.

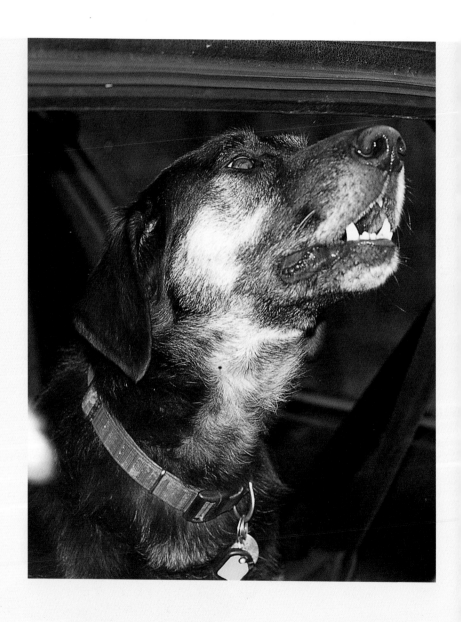

Chapter 1

Dealing with aggression

Aggression is a normal, natural way for dogs to keep themselves safe or to try to resolve disputes. They cannot reason with their attacker or opponent or get their solicitor involved, and therefore they take the only option that is open to them when something upsets them. The answer to aggression problems lies in finding out the underlying reason for the aggressive behaviour and solving the problems for the dog before the dog tries to solve the problems for itself.

Causes and solutions

Aggression towards people is often due to dogs perceiving themselves to be under threat and reacting to try to keep themselves safe. There is always a reason why dogs show aggression and finding that reason is the key to the solution.

Many dogs are fearful because they did not grow accustomed to people when they were puppies. Dogs do not need to have bad experiences – just a lack of experience with different people of all ages and personalities when puppies are between the critical socialization ages of three to twelve weeks.

Fearful factors

Under-socialized dogs will be fearful of strangers and will only feel safe with family members whom they have learned to trust. Some under-socialized dogs will be okay with adults but will be very fearful of children. Lack of good experiences with children during puppyhood can result in a fear of children that leads to aggression. Children are faster

▼ Fearful dogs will need some time to overcome their concerns slowly in a safe environment. This low, sideways non-threatening posture with averted eyes helps this Collie to gather the courage to come forward.

moving, have more high-pitched voices and are smaller than adults. Consequently, they can seem very scary to some dogs that readily learn that being aggressive keeps them away.

Some dogs have had bad experiences with people. These may be strangers who have frightened or hurt them, even unwittingly. Dogs have long memories and are particularly impressionable during puppyhood. If the dog fails to have good experiences with these people or people like them to make up for this, then they may be afraid that they will be hurt or scared by this type of person again.

Similarly, some dogs may be hurt or frightened by their owners. Unknowledgeable owners often punish their dog to try to train it. This rarely teaches the dog how to behave but it does damage the dog's trust and he may learn to be aggressive to get his owners to stop the punishment.

Dogs that have been frightened or hurt by people will usually be afraid of, and hence aggressive towards, specific people or actions as, for example, when a person raises a hand quickly above their head, when a person is drunk, or when an owner is cross and has sent the dog to his bed. Often the dog will link together all the circumstances that were present when he was frightened or hurt and will become aggressive when these particular trigger factors occur again.

Confident dogs

To be aggressive, a dog needs to have confidence. Well-bred puppies rarely show real aggression until they are about seven months old when they begin to have more confidence in their own abilities. A dog may be more confident, and hence more likely to show aggression, when he is with his owner or confined in a small space, such as a car. Dogs that have strong characters, such as the guarding breeds, are more likely to have the confidence to show aggression. The feisty terrier breeds are quick to show aggression, biting first and thinking later, as was required when their ancestors faced large adversaries, such as badgers and foxes, in their lairs. Sharp, reactive breeds, such as Collies, are usually more sensitive and, hence, more prone to fears that other breeds. They often lack confidence, and thus will usually snap or bite and then move away.

Dogs that growl, snarl or lunge forward aggressively without making any contact are usually trying to scare people away. Dogs are often as accurate with their mouths as we are with our hands, and if they mean to make contact, they will do so. These threat displays are frequently loud and explosive as this gives them their best chance of frightening off their 'attacker'. If this does not work and people keep approaching, or the person approaches too fast for warnings to be given, the dog may have to resort to biting. Dogs cannot ask you nicely to stay away, so they have to find another way. Most people either do not read a dog's fearful body language, or they take no notice. Instead, they continue to approach until the dog is forced to take action. Dogs often get punished for making early warning signs, such as growling, until eventually they no longer show them. Consequently, they are likely to bite without warning instead which can be very dangerous.

Solving the problem

Once dogs have learned to use aggression to keep people away, owners need professional help from a pet behaviour counsellor to overcome the problem safely. To help dogs get over their fear of people, they need to have carefully controlled gradual, repeated exposure to one person until

they have made friends, learned to trust them and enjoy their company. Once this has happened 10 times with different people, most dogs begin to generalize and realize that people are safe to be with. However, this can take a very long time and requires plenty of patience. A good owner who will take charge without being overbearing is essential as the dog will need to learn to rely on them for guidance and security.

◀ Towering over a dog in this way with full eye contact and a raised hand causes this undersocialized dog to be worried. He puts his ears and tail down, moves back over his hind legs ready to run if necessary and barks a warning not to come closer.

Questions and Answers

Q We have had our Lancashire Heeler, Jasper, for eight years. Recently, he has become aggressive, and has tried to bite us on four separate occasions during the last six months. We are becoming somewhat wary of him and would not feel comfortable leaving him in anyone else's care. What can we do?

A If he has been well behaved for eight years and has only recently become aggressive, it is important that you get him thoroughly checked out by your veterinary surgeon as there could be something wrong with him that is causing him to be bad tempered. This is the usual reason for dogs that have been well behaved becoming snappy. However, it could also be due to changes in circumstances. Have you moved house recently, had any additions to the family, changed his routine, or has he had any other experiences that could have made him react in this way? If the answer is 'no' to all of these questions, it brings us back to physical problems in his body being the most likely cause for changes in his behaviour.

Q Every time that I try to brush my Yorkshire Terrier's tangled fur he goes for me, becomes very upset and shakes a lot. How can I solve this problem?

A The hairs in a Yorkie's coat are fine and easily tangled and the skin is very sensitive. So you probably frequently hurt him without realizing. Since he cannot say, 'Ouch, that hurts!', he has to put up with it until it gets too much. This is why he shakes – he will be anticipating the pain, be upset that he has to be aggressive with his friend, and will probably also be worried that you will get cross.

To overcome this, try to groom very small sections, perhaps two to

▶ Get your dog accustomed to being groomed and do it regularly to prevent tangles forming in the coat.

three times a day for a few minutes. Be very gentle and hold the base of the hair firmly if you are teasing out a knot so that you don't pull his skin. End sessions with fun, dinner or a walk and keep the sessions going until you have groomed him all over. If his coat is very knotty, then you may have to consider having him clipped out by a vet or groomer. Once this is done, it will be very easy for you to brush him and win his confidence.

The secret is patience and imagining what it feels like to be him. You could also try bathing him with a special shampoo which is designed to prevent tangles in children's hair, or spraying on a coat conditioner that will make the hairs slip over each other more easily, making him easier to groom.

Q *Jake is a one-year-old German Shepherd Dog whom we rescued four months ago. He had been kept in a small kennel and we believe he had been beaten. He is great with the family but would eat anyone else! He is very close to my husband, Billy, and behaves more aggressively when they are together. A behaviourist has been working with us for about four weeks now and there has been some progress. She is trying to reduce the bond between Billy and Jake, and teach Jake to accept new people more readily. Sometimes we seem to be winning with him, then suddenly he seems to go backwards. The behaviourist can only work with Jake when he is muzzled and says that we cannot rush things. What do you think?*

A Unfortunately, there is no quick, easy way to overcome fears, especially those that are caused by lack of adequate socialization or by mistreatment during puppyhood. Slow but sure is the only way. You can expect little setbacks along the way, so don't raise your hopes too

▶ Territorial aggression is due to lack of trust and fear of intruders

high too quickly. As long as you have made some progress at the end of each week, that is enough. Muzzles are necessary to start with to prevent injury, but your dog should never be pushed so far that he is forced to show aggression. The only way to overcome fear-based aggression is to systematically desensitize Jake to the things of which he is scared, pairing small amounts of things that worry him with lots of pleasant experiences to help him realize that people are good news rather than bad.

Q *My Dobermann has a tendency to growl or try to bite me when I say 'no' to him – for example, when he is playing with one of my shoes. What should I do about this?*

A Dobermanns tend to have strong natures and it is not uncommon for them to want to rule the pack if they get a chance. If he has been challenging you over other issues, such as getting off beds or sofas, lying in doorways or being groomed, it is possible that he is trying to take control. You will need advice from a pet behaviour counsellor to stop this from escalating and to learn how to become a more effective leader. (This isn't done by intimidation but by a system of winning encounters.)

Alternatively, if you have used threats or intimidation to retrieve objects from him in the past, it could be that he is simply protecting himself. Dogs usually begin to assert themselves when they are about seven months old, and if you used force to get him to do things for you when he was a puppy, then he may have grown into a defensive dog that growls and snaps when you frighten him. It is probably best to see a specialist before this gets out of hand.

Food guarding

Dogs may feel they need to guard food as it is a valued resource that may be scarce, or has been in the past, and they don't want to go hungry. Food guarders feel that they need to protect their food in order to survive, even if this is not actually true.

Food guarding usually begins with the dog just growling, then escalating to snarling and even snapping in the air as a threat if the owner's hands come closer. If these warnings are ignored, and the dog has enough confidence, or the hands approach too quickly, bites may result.

   If the owner punishes such behaviour, the aggression can escalate quickly as the dog is now also becoming worried about aggression from the owner. If the punishment from the owner is severe enough, the aggression can be suppressed, but it may come out later, unexpectedly and with severity, with a person who is perceived as weaker, especially children or visitors.

Preventing the problem

In puppies, we can prevent food aggression by teaching them that hands come to give, not take away. This is done by luring them away from what they are eating with a titbit that is much smellier and tastier than the food they are eating. While they are concentrating on this, the food or chew they were eating can be removed. The titbit is then given to them before the food or chew is replaced. If this

▶ Feeding puppies from the same bowl causes them to compete for food which can teach them how to be aggressive over food from an early age. Feeding each puppy from a separate bowl helps prevent this.

happens regularly, the puppy will soon learn that human hands come to give rather than take, and so there is no need to be aggressive to keep them away.

Solving the problem

If your dog is growling, biting, snapping or attacking over food, you will need professional help from a pet behaviour counsellor in order to solve the problem safely and successfully. The solution lies in teaching the dog that approaching human hands are good news rather than bad, but this needs to be done very carefully. It is important to treat this problem rather than just managing it in case someone, particularly a child, approaches unexpectedly one day while the dog is eating.

Until you can get help, you could try hand feeding, feeding in a different place, scatter feeding which reduces the amount of food in one place, and placing food inside strong toys so that your dog has to work to get it out. Care should be taken to leave the dog alone while he eats until you are able to tackle the problem with a professional.

As well as making sure that your dog is safe around food, it is also important that he should learn not to guard bones and chews. This needs to be done in a similar way, patiently teaching him that your hands are coming to give, not take. Until you are able to do this, it is a good idea to give many chews or bones so that each becomes less valuable, or to give chews and bones only when he is shut in a room or the garden. Alternatively, do not give chews or bones at all if you cannot keep him safely shut away while he chews them.

▶ This dog means business and has learned to bite to protect his food. Many owners escalate food aggression by becoming threatening when the dog gives a warning growl.

Questions and Answers

Q *Six months ago, we gave a home to an eight-year-old Pointer called Barney. He looked thin and had to have two teeth extracted due to a huge abscess in his mouth. He has a tendency to bite us when we try to put our hands near his head, although other parts of his body can be approached without trouble. He prefers me to my husband and is very protective over his food, indeed so much so that my husband has to stay out of the way when Barney is eating as he growls and snarls if he walks past.*

A Dogs that bite usually have a very good reason to do so and it is not hard to imagine Barney trying to protect himself from the intense pain caused by people touching his face when he had tooth abscesses, especially if he had little trust in his previous owners. When pain is very intense, it tends to leave very deep impressions and anything associated with that pain will be remembered long after the reason for that pain has been taken away.

If Barney is biting in earnest, then you will need to seek professional help from a pet behaviour counsellor to ensure that you do not get bitten and injured during the desensitization process. This will require you to teach Barney that your hands come to bring good things rather than pain, and will help you gradually gain his trust so that he learns that your hands will never hurt him. You will need professional help to ensure that you read his signals correctly while you do this and do not push him to the point at which he feels threatened and reacts defensively. Properly done, this desensitization process can achieve some remarkable results in a relatively short time, and the end result will be a trust between you that will make both of you feel better.

In a similar way, it is likely that Barney growls whenever your husband walks past his food bowl because a man has been aggressive to him when he was eating or he has had to fight for enough to eat at some time in his life. The simplest way to deal with this is to put him in a room on his own when he is eating and call him out of there when he has finished so that you can go in to pick up the bowl. Later, when Barney has learned to trust you, ask your pet behaviour counsellor to help you devise a special treatment programme to teach him that hands come to give while he is eating, rather than take.

CASE HISTORY

Aggression to children

Dog: Jimmy, Staffordshire Bull Terrier, two years, entire male

Background

At only five weeks old, Jimmy was stolen, along with the rest of his litter from the breeder's kennels. Somehow he became separated from his litter mates and was walking alone down a London street when he was hit accidentally by a lorry. The lorry driver rushed him to Battersea Dogs Home where they cared for him until he was well enough to be adopted by the driver of the lorry, who had been visiting him regularly since the accident.

Jimmy settled down well in his new home. He was friendly with everyone, including any visiting children, and played well with them. So it was a shock to the owner when, at one year old, Jimmy started being explosively and uncharacteristically aggressive to children, lunging and barking at them both at home and in the street.

It was difficult to know why the aggression had started and so all the possibilities were examined to try to find the root cause. Behaviour problems that have a sudden onset are often connected with a medical condition, and it was a

▶ Jimmy was lucky to have an owner who cared enough about him to help him get over his fear of children.

surprise that the vet could find nothing wrong. Jimmy's encounters with children were always supervised and there was no possibility that he had been teased. His owners were kind and loving and had never punished him. It was hard to find a reason for the unexpected aggression until, one week after the consultation, his owner went outside to call Jimmy in and found four young boys leaning over the fence at the bottom of the garden, calling Jimmy and throwing exploding caps down in front of his paws. This terrified Jimmy who was barking furiously. The owner visited the neighbours and put a stop to it. For some time, Jimmy lost confidence with adults as well as children and if anyone tried to look him in the eye, he would get scared, lungeing and barking.

Treatment plan

The programme began with getting Jimmy to overcome his fear of adults before working with children. This involved a slow and gradual exposure to strangers so that he could learn to trust them again. They always brought tasty treats and toys to play with so the fear could be turned into interest and enjoyment. At first they avoided all eye contact as that was the trigger that caused Jimmy to react aggressively. Once the owner had worked on eye contact exercises and had taught him that it was safe to be stared at, Jimmy's new 'friends' did the same exercises, rewarding him with a titbit or a game whenever they caught his eye, gradually teaching him to hold the eye contact for longer until he overcame his fear.

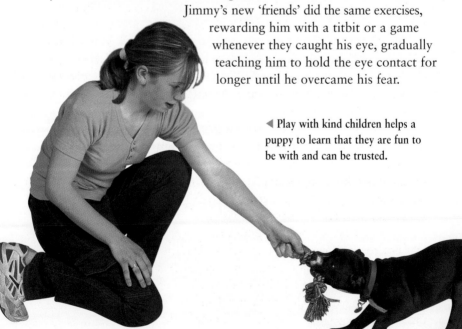

◀ Play with kind children helps a puppy to learn that they are fun to be with and can be trusted.

Outcome

The owner worked very hard to overcome Jimmy's concerns, firstly by introducing him to women and later to men. Gradually, and carefully, children were allowed to visit again. After about two years of intensive treatment, Jimmy got much better. If he became worried when strangers were in the house, he would pick up his favourite toy and go to his bed until he calmed down, returning later when he felt braver. This letter from Jimmy's owners shows how far he has come since those early days when he would explode into ferocious barking at the sight of a child.

Just before Christmas, I was shopping in town with my girlfriend. I gave Jimmy to my girlfriend to look after while I went into a shop. As usual he was carrying his Frisbee in his mouth as it seems to take his mind off things happening around him and acts as a sort of comforter. They sat down together outside the shop and Jimmy laid his Frisbee on the floor upside down.

My girlfriend was watching for me coming out of the shop and was not paying any attention to Jimmy. Unseen by her, a toddler wandered over to Jimmy, patted him on the head, put a sausage roll in his mouth, and a coin in his Frisbee. The toddler's parents must have thought that my girlfriend and Jimmy were homeless! Jimmy didn't bat an eyelid; he just ate the sausage roll.

Chapter 2

Home alone

Some dogs may be destructive, noisy or messy when left alone, which can be very frustrating for owners, many of whom will punish their dogs on their return. Since this punishment occurs long after the event, the dog cannot learn from this. Although he can remember what he did earlier, if the owner punishes him later, he cannot connect the two things and so will not learn. However, dogs will learn rapidly to associate their returning owner's anger with punishment, and they will show submission in an attempt to appease the owner. Some owners often misinterpret this behaviour as 'looking guilty' and punish the dog more.

Fear of isolation

To find a cure for separation problems, we need to discover why the dog does what he does. Different problems will have slightly different symptoms, and these can be used as clues to help identify the cause behind the behaviour which will lead us to the most appropriate cure.

Isolation is an unnatural state for dogs, and if they find themselves alone they will attempt to reunite themselves with their pack. Some dogs have not learned to tolerate isolation, and therefore being left alone is a frightening experience for them. This problem is particularly common in newly rescued dogs that have been abandoned once by their owners.

Symptoms

The dog may whine or bark, sniff under the door, push, scratch or chew at the bottom of the door, the carpet or door frames in an effort to get through. He may run around the house or room, looking for a way out, and may jump up on windowsills, knocking things off surfaces as he

does so. If the dog manages to get out of the house, he will go looking for someone to be with. He may even be upset enough to defecate and urinate in the house. If this state continues, then many small runny piles

◀ Finding themselves home alone without the protection of their owners can be worrying for dogs that have not learned to cope with it. Leaving puppies alone for short, gradually increasing periods will help them learn to accept isolation.

of faeces are likely to be deposited. After about 15 minutes, however, the dog will begin to calm down slightly. Dogs with this problem are happy provided that someone (anyone!) is with them.

Solutions

■ You should always exercise your dog well in advance of him being left on his own.

■ Keep the time that you spend making departure preparations (collecting keys, putting on coats, closing windows, etc.) to the absolute minimum. You should try to get ready earlier if necessary.

■ You should ignore your dog for half an hour before going out.

■ Leave your dog in a familiar place where any damage done will be minimal (well away from danger and valuables), or where his barking is least likely to annoy your neighbours. Alternatively, you should leave your dog with a friend or a relative until the following programme is completed.

▲ Dogs that fear isolation will try to find a way out of the house to be with people.

Home alone programme

1 Teach your dog to tolerate being left alone by giving him gradually increasing periods of isolation. Always start off with a length of time that the dog can cope with, even if it is just a few seconds. Repeat this a few times during each session with many sessions a day.

2 Build up the time that the dog can tolerate being alone gradually over many sessions over several days, never going faster than he can cope with.

3 Once the dog can cope with being left for an hour while you are in a different part of the house, repeat this procedure but, this time, leave the house. Begin with very short absences as before, gradually building them up.

> **Note:** Do not leave your dog in a cage with the door shut as this can result in injuries to the mouth and paws as he makes frantic efforts to escape.

Questions and Answers

Q I recently purchased Ollie, a two-year-old Bichon Frise, as a companion for my mother. Unfortunately, he has various behavioural problems of which the biggest is that he doesn't like to be left alone. I am trying to keep him in isolation for periods of time when I am in the house and he is coping with this, but if I leave the house he barks and whines uncontrollably.

A Dogs are intensely social animals and they need to be trained to tolerate isolation. It sounds as though your mother's dog may not have learned to be alone and may also have some fear-based problems. You should continue with your planned programme of separation, leaving him only for short periods that cause him no distress and gradually building them up. Once he can be alone without worrying for 30 minutes, begin to leave the house, but initially for just a few minutes before returning, gradually lengthening the time until he can cope with this, too.

▶ Saying effusive goodbyes just before leaving can be counter-productive since the contrast between being together and being apart may seem even greater.

Q *Until two weeks ago I had two Westies, but Jock died when he was 15 and now I am left with Robbie. I understand how he misses Jock; they'd been together for 14 years. Robbie's started chewing the door frame when I leave him to go to work. Could you give me any advice? I don't want him to be unhappy.*

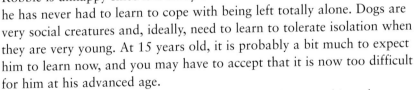

A I'm sorry that you have lost Jock after all those years with him. It is not surprising that Robbie is unhappy since it is likely that he has never had to learn to cope with being left totally alone. Dogs are very social creatures and, ideally, need to learn to tolerate isolation when they are very young. At 15 years old, it is probably a bit much to expect him to learn now, and you may have to accept that it is now too difficult for him at his advanced age.

However, if you were at home all the time and not working, then you could gradually lengthen the time he is left alone until he can cope with longer absences. If you go out to work for long periods of time, you will not be able to do this, and I suggest that you find someone who would be able to look after him during the day, either permanently or while you teach him to be left alone.

Unfortunately, getting another dog is probably not a good option. Although it may be company for Robbie, it would not be the same as having Jock with him and you may find that he passes on his distress at being left to the new dog so that you have double the trouble.

Home alone tip

Teaching dogs to be left alone needs to be done slowly. Until they can cope, try to arrange for them to stay with a friend or relative, or even as a day boarder in a kennels until they find it easier to be alone at home.

CASE HISTORY

The barker

Dog: Winston, German Short-haired Pointer, six months, entire male

Background

Winston was kept in a shed in the garden by his original owners. He had been bought as a present for a 16-year-old boy who spent very little time with him. He was passed on to a new home at the age of five months but, after only four days, the new owners no longer wanted him either and gave him to his present family.

When put out into the garden, Winston ran round the house looking for a way in. Eventually he settled by the back door but set up a loud, regular bark. This bark is driven by anxiety and dogs can keep it up for hours. If left alone in the house, Winston would do exactly the same thing, having tried frantically to get out by scratching at the door and door frames. The previous owners had shut him into a wire cage to try to prevent him doing this and, as a direct result, Winston had to have veterinary treatment to the injuries to his mouth and front paws which had been caused by his frenzied efforts to escape.

Treatment plan

Arrangements were made for Winston to be left with a friend or relative if his owner had to go out until the treatment was completed to prevent him getting worried about being alone.

Get him used to being alone slowly

Winston was kept behind a stair gate while he got used to his owner moving slowly into other parts of the house. Once he tolerated this happily, his owner began to close the door, leaving him shut in and alone for just a few seconds before returning. Over several sessions, she gradually extended the time for which she was absent and always proceeded at a speed that Winston could cope with. Once he could be left on his own for half an hour with no problem, the process was begun again, but this time he was left in the house alone.

Outcome

The treatment has been very successful and Winston is now able to settle down quietly by himself in the house whenever the owner is out.

Other fears

Dogs will often develop separation problems if they are afraid of something. The fear can be of something inside the house, for example, the heating switching on and off, in which case the dog may try to escape. Once outside, he may be quite happy to sit in the garden and will not wander away; he just does not want to be inside with the source of the fear.

Alternatively, a dog may sometimes be frightened of something outside, such as dustbin collections, other dogs or strangers. It is not uncommon for a dog to develop fear-related problems after a break-in that has occurred while he was alone in the house.

Symptoms

Although they may destroy some items within the house, fearful dogs are unlikely to be noisy since this would draw attention to themselves. Some dogs will selectively chew things that smell of their owners, often choosing things that smell of one owner in particular. After chewing the item into shreds, they usually curl up in the centre of the debris as they seem to feel more safe if surrounded by their owner's scent. In a similar

▲ Chewing things that smell of the owner, such as clothing and tissues, help to reassure the dog and enable him to surround himself with a barrier of his owner's scent.

▶ When dog and owner spend almost all of the time together, they are both likely to become very attached. This can cause problems when they are separated, even for a very short time.

way, some dogs will mark all strategic points with their urine as soon as the owner goes out to enable them to feel more secure in the territory. They may also try to dig a 'den' in a sofa, cupboard, bed or the carpet.

Solutions

Until you find a solution, wear a large, old sweater or a T-shirt before leaving, and put it in the place where the dog lies when you are out. You will need to renew the scent on this garment each time you leave the house. Create a den in the favourite sleeping place using a covered table or a wire cage (door left *open*) or large cardboard box.

The long-term answer to this problem lies in finding out what it is that the dog is afraid of and treating that fear. Gradual exposure to the fear-inducing experience, together with the timely provision of games and food to encourage him to enjoy the experience, will change his attitude from fear to acceptance. For example, if he is afraid of people, a socialization programme will be necessary to encourage him to be more comfortable with them. If he has a phobia, an intensive treatment programme will be needed to get him over this. Sometimes, the removal of the fear-inducing stimulus may be a simpler solution. For example, you could leave a dog who is frightened of the noise of the central heating boiler switching on and off in the living room, not the kitchen.

◀ A covered kennel with the door left open can become a safe den-like retreat for some dogs, particularly if it is placed where they feel most secure.

Too attached

If the relationship between the owner and dog is very intense, another person may be no substitute for the owner. Some owners engender more emotional attachment in dogs than others, and then it is necessary for both owners and dogs to become more independent.

You can begin by giving your dog 'dollops' of attention rather than a continuous trickle, say for five minutes in every half an hour. During the 25 minutes that he is not getting attention it is important to ignore him completely by not speaking, looking or talking to him. Gradually increase this time until he can cope with getting no attention for one hour; then it is time to begin short periods of real separation (see page 25).

In extreme cases, where the dog has been in constant physical contact with the owner, for example, by sitting on their lap or touching their foot, he needs to learn to accept being just out of contact for short periods of time. To do this, fasten him to a fixed object just out of your range and increase the distance gradually over many sessions.

▶ Ignoring the dog's demands for attention is the first step towards independence. It is important to give just as much attention as you usually do, but it should be your choice rather than the dog's decision.

Questions and Answers

Q *Shotzee is a hunting dog who is kept in an outdoor/indoor kennel. Several months ago, he had a barking fit that lasted for approximately two hours. These fits are becoming more and more frequent and do not respond to anything that my husband and I do. What could have caused them in an otherwise quiet and obedient dog?*

A I suspect that something has scared him sufficiently for him to try to seek protection from his owners. Barking that lasts for two hours is usually driven by anxiety, unless an 'intruder' is prowling for that length of time, and he might have been trying to attract your attention in the hope that you would make him feel more safe. It is up to you to find out what frightened him, but it could be a noise or someone or something that is worrying him. Usually, it will take one or two incidences with something frightening to cause a dog to become anxious.

Now that he is sensitized to it, a smaller amount of the stimulus will set him off. Each time, he will become more anxious, which is why the barking sessions are getting more frequent. Generally, problems like this are accentuated by illness or old age. I would suggest that you visit your veterinary surgeon in order to check that all is well. I would also recommend that Shotzee comes into the house to sleep for a while so that he feels he has the protection of his 'pack'.

Failure to do this is likely to accentuate the problem, and it will get

◀ Solitary confinement in a kennel can be traumatic for many social dogs, particularly if there is something worrying in their environment.

even worse. Once he has settled down again and got his confidence back, then Shotzee can be reintroduced to his kennel gradually, but you may have to desensitize him to his fear of the unknown thing first.

Q *Our puppy, Arnold, is 10 months old and urinates all over the house. He cocks his leg on all the furniture, curtains, beds, clothes etc. He only seems to do it when we are either out or in bed. He does not have an infection, but the house is now starting to smell because of him. We have to wash the curtains and scrub the couch regularly and he is even making our wooden floor lift. We have put up with it until now but, with a new baby on the way, it will be very unhygienic. Our vet has suggested an indoor kennel, but I don't think I could find one big enough. Do you have any ideas or suggestions?*

A If your dog is doing it only when he is left alone, then it could be that he is feeling insecure and worried without his protective pack leaders. Marking his territory with urine would make him feel better. If this is the cause, it is likely that Arnold will mark strategic points at the entrances to rooms and around the doorways. Usually, only a small amount of urine is used to mark, but it will be enough to cause a noticeable smell over a period of time. If large amounts of urine are left, then it could be a housetraining problem, and an indoor kennel may cause more problems than it solves.

If it is a fear-based problem, then your dog may panic and may even cause himself some damage. However, if it is a housetraining probem, then it may force Arnold to get accustomed to lying in his own mess.

The first thing to do is clean the areas thoroughly with some biological washing powder solution to remove the smell. Allow to dry and then wipe over with surgical spirit (do a patch test first in case colours run). Shut Arnold into one room to reduce the areas that become soiled, and get help to solve the problem.

CASE HISTORY

The milk bottle smasher

Dog: Leo, German Shepherd cross, three years, neutered male

Background

Leo had been passed through three homes before arriving at his latest owners and was described by his new owner as a 'sensitive, loving boy'. However, he was less than loving with strangers and would put up a spirited defence of his property, showing that he viewed all strangers as a threat. Leo was left in the kitchen when the owner when out to work. At first, he pulled down tea towels and the owner would return to find them shredded in his bed. When she put these away in a drawer, Leo moved on to taking mugs. She finally decided to seek advice when, after leaving three milk bottles in the sink, she came home to find them smashed all over the kitchen floor.

Treatment plan

A plan was devised was to help Leo feel more safe when he was left alone at home. A temporary 'den' was constructed by putting his bed under the kitchen table and hanging a large, heavy tablecloth so that he was enclosed. Every day before leaving, the owner left a recently worn T-shirt in his bed for him to curl up in. Leo was carefully introduced to a number of the owner's friends who gave him plenty of tasty treats and games with toys and visited regularly until he began to see them as friends instead of enemies.

Outcome

Eventually Leo became much more settled and friendly to strangers and stopped taking things off the kitchen surfaces.

◀ Hiding underneath the table and curling up in something that smells of the owner can help to give a frightened dog a feeling of security.

Boredom and bad habits

Leaving an active dog alone all day can lead to a variety of problem behaviours. Usually dogs that do not mind being left will lie down and sleep at first.

If owners are out for long, the dog may chew items he should not have because there is nothing else to do. In these cases, he usually returns to the same site each time or to items made of the same material. Alternatively, he may amuse himself by barking at every disturbance outside, however slight. Boredom is more likely to occur in young dogs and in those with very active minds, usually the working breeds.

Solutions

1 Give your dog plenty of exercise when you are at home, especially just before leaving the house. You should provide physical exercise and also mental exercise in the form of training and games.

2 If you leave your dog for long stretches of time, you should arrange for someone to come in halfway through the day to provide stimulation and an opportunity to exercise.

3 Leave novelty chews and bones. Provide 'new' ones every day of the week so all chewing is focused on the 'novelty' items. Remove them when you come home.

◀ Plenty of exercise when you are at home will help to prevent dogs from becoming problematic when left alone at home.

Trying to get the owner to return

Some dogs become frustrated if they are not able to follow their owner, but although these dogs are aroused and excited, they are not necessarily afraid or anxious. They may try chewing many different items that brought them attention from their owner in the past.

This relies on the dog learning that you will only come back to him when he is behaving in the way that you desire, i.e. lying down quietly. In the same way as for fear of isolation, it will be necessary to teach the dog to tolerate gradually increasing periods of isolation (see page 25).

▲ Providing plenty of different types of chew will make it less likely that your dog will chew things he should not.

Frustration

Damage to the interior of a house may result from a situation where the dog has an opportunity to observe events that are going on outside but is denied the opportunity to join in. This is especially common in those

situations where the dog would like to see off canine or human intruders to the property but is denied the chance to do so. The aggression is often redirected onto soft furnishings instead. In these cases, there will usually be some vocalization, often in the form of barking or whining, during any periods of excitement which can become a problem if you have neighbours close by.

◀ Damage around windows is commonly caused by dogs that are frustrated at not being able to join in with exciting events going on outside.

CASE HISTORY

The shoe eater

Dog: Seal, Labrador cross, eight months, female

Background

The whole family of two parents, four children (aged between three and eight years) and Seal arrived for the consultation. When they were asked about the nature of the problem, they told me that Seal had already chewed and mostly eaten 11 pairs of shoes since they had acquired her only two months earlier. They said that much as they loved him, it was getting expensive. All four children were wearing brand new shoes!

Treatment plan

A treatment plan was devised on the premise that the family must appreciate that Seal needed to chew. As an adolescent, she needed to explore and also to exercise her jaws and therefore she would have a strong desire to chew until she reached maturity. Providing alternative things to chew, such as large, strong rubber toys, would keep her away from shoes. Toys were made more interesting by stuffing them with her food, cream cheese and peanut butter. Plenty of safe, suitable chews were provided each day and kept interesting by allowing her to have two of them for just one day before replacing them with different ones.

Keep Seal away from shoes!

Until Seal learnt not to chew shoes, a special place was used inside a cupboard where shoes were stored when not on feet. A stair gate was employed to keep Seal downstairs so he did not have access to the landing where shoes were frequently left.

Outcome

Seal soon learned to enjoy chewing her strong, chewable toys instead of shoes, and thus the bill for footwear in her household was greatly reduced.

Chapter 3

Sex-related problems

Sex-related problems begin at puberty when the reproductive hormones begin circulating. In some dogs, these changes can actually lead to behaviour problems due to their natural desire to reproduce and pass on their genes to the next generation. They may escape, roam, mount objects, people or other animals, and scent mark. Not all dogs have such sex-related problems but some seem to have more interest in these activities. These problems can usually be solved by neutering, although careful consideration is necessary in order to distinguish them from problems with similar symptoms but a different cause.

Escaping and roaming

Until you have found a solution to the problem of escaping, tightened security is essential to prevent your dog getting out and perhaps being injured in an accident (you are liable financially if your dog causes an accident when outside). However, a determined dog will usually find a way to get out or will wait for an opportune moment to slip through an open door so a solution needs to be found quickly.

Bitches come into season approximately twice a year and may try to get out at this time in order to find a mate, particularly around the tenth day of their season. Entire dogs will often escape to get to bitches in season. Males can smell a bitch in season from three miles away so in a built-up area it is likely that there may always be a bitch to visit. It is important to distinguish between this and other reasons for dogs escaping and wandering off. Their lives may be more exciting away from home or they may be trying to escape from frightening events, such as aggressive owners or some teasing children.

Discovering the cause

To find out the cause of your dog's behaviour, you need to discover where he goes and what he does when he gets out. He may go wandering in some woods, fields and parks or try to find other dogs, adults or children to play with. If a male dog camps out outside the

▶ Both bitches and dogs will try to escape to find mating partners. Dogs will do this when they can smell a bitch in season, whereas bitches will do this during the later part of their season when they are ready to mate.

◀ Raising the leg enables the dog to leave a chemical message at nose height for other dogs to read. This will give them a lot of information, such as state of health and sexual status.

▶ Dogs that escape from home to find mating partners may roam for several miles and cover a wide area. However, during this time, they run the risk of being involved in road traffic accidents.

home of a bitch in season, then neutering may be the answer. If a bitch stays at home most of the time but makes determined efforts to escape during her seasons, neutering may, again, be necessary.

If your dog is escaping and running away from home because his life is more exciting elsewhere, then it is important that you play together frequently throughout the day. You should make a positive effort to rebuild the relationship you have with your dog, teach him tricks and train him with rewards. It is easy to forget and ignore a well-behaved dog, and you should work out a structured plan so that you spend more time with him throughout the day. Fun times need to come at random so that your dog cannot predict when they will happen, and this will keep him waiting around in anticipation.

CASE HISTORY

The clothes-line thief

Dog: Bill, German Shepherd cross, five years, entire male

Background

Bill lived on a farm in a village and, since a puppy, had been allowed complete freedom to go where he pleased. When he was young, he had stayed close to home, but gradually his wanderings took him further afield. Since the village was quiet without much traffic and he did not chase livestock, the owners had allowed this. All the neighbours knew him and if they had a bitch in season and he turned up at their home, they would call his owners who would collect him. He was known to have fathered at least one litter of puppies in the village.

All was well until a new family moved into the village. Soon after they arrived, they noticed items of clothing were going missing from their washing line. They were pegged out to dry in the morning but when the owner came home in the afternoon, she was unnerved to find that some of the larger items had been taken. When this happened on the third day in a row, she called the police. That evening the owner noticed a big black dog in the garden. She phoned the number on his collar and Bill's owners came to collect him. She explained that her Boxer bitch was in season and Bill's owners promised to keep him inside for a few weeks.

The following day, Bill escaped again and his owner, noticing that he had gone and knowing just where he would be found, went to collect him. She found him in the Boxer's owner's back garden, lying on a T-shirt that he had pulled off the washing line. However, as she went towards him, he growled, then picked up the T-shirt and ran off. When she eventually caught up with him in some nearby woods, he was sitting on a stash of clothing. When the Boxer's owner returned

◀ Waiting outside the door for a bitch in season is not unusual for entire males; they may be there for days.

home later that day, Bill's owner took the pile of clothes round and was embarrassed to confess that her dog was the culprit.

Observations and diagnosis

Dogs live in a world dominated by scent, whereas for us sight is our most important sense. Bitches in oestrus emit a powerful scent designed to attract entire male dogs and lead them to their door. This scent would have spread onto the Boxer's coat and, as the owner stroked her dog, it would have been transferred to her hands. From there it would have spread to the washing as she pegged it onto the line. For Bill, who was frustratedly sitting outside all day longing to get to the Boxer in the house, the larger items of clothing within easy reach would have been the next best thing. Pulling them down off the line would not have been difficult but it is hard to say why he would have taken them off

▲ Items that smell of a bitch in season can become important objects that need to be kept safe.

into the woods. Perhaps an earlier memory of being scolded for stealing things off the washing line, a popular pastime for puppies looking for something moving to play with, might have told him not to hang around in the garden afterwards. Bitches in season are valuable possessions to be looked after and guarded, and perhaps Bill was doing this with the clothes.

Treatment plan

The owner had two choices: either to manage Bill as she had always done by keeping him at home when bitches were in season or have him castrated. Bill had been known to travel many miles in order to find bitches in season, often crossing two major roads. This, together with the knowledge that there was now another entire bitch in the village, prompted his owners to decide to have him castrated.

Outcome

After being neutered, Bill stopped running off to find bitches in season and became a much more relaxed and home-loving dog.

Mounting

Puppies will often play-mount moving things when they become excited. This is normal and allows them to practise in case they need to use this behaviour in later life.

Mounting in male dogs begins in earnest when they reach puberty. Their levels of testosterone soar and consequently male puppies will show mounting behaviour more frequently than adults, mounting anything as the mood takes them. For most dogs, this desire settles down as they mature. However, for others, the desire to mate and mount will remain high. Small children bending over are often a target, as are people's legs, stuffed toys and cushions.

Solutions
1 With puppies, you should gently stop any mounting behaviour, or ignore it if possible and try not to worry until the puppy grows up!
2 For older dogs, you should gently remove the dog from company so that people can calm down and he is not rewarded by excited attention. If he gets aggressive when stopped, consider castration and get advice from a pet behaviour counsellor to help you reassess your relationship.

▼ Courtship is often very brief if the female is ready for mating. Mounting quickly follows a brief bout of play.

◀ Mounting behaviour may be used to subdue other dogs. Here a female mounts another in an effort to impress on her that she is at the bottom of the hierarchy.

3 Talk to your veterinary surgeon about having your dog castrated. This will stop the unwanted behaviour if it is driven by sexual urges, and he will be less frustrated (see page 48).

Play mounting

For some dogs, particularly those that are undersocialized, mounting games may continue long after puppyhood as they do not know how to play other types of games. They can usually be distracted onto games with toys instead, and the mounting behaviour reduces considerably once they know how to play more satisfying games with people and other dogs.

Controlling behaviour

Both male and female dogs can sometimes use mounting behaviour to control others. Some dogs may stand on the shoulders of others when they meet and transform this into mounting behaviour if they can. This seems to be a way for each of the parties to assess the confidence of the other.

   Between dogs living in the same household, mounting behaviour is often used by the top-ranking dog in order to control or suppress the underdog. It is particularly used after a transgression of the hierarchy rules and is a way of putting the other dog in its place without resorting to aggression.

   When it is done to excess or used against people, this behaviour should be treated more seriously. During conflicts with owners, some dogs may try to mount their legs or they may attempt to mount children if they are having problems with them. Attempts to stop this may be met with aggression. If this occurs, then it is time to get some professional advice to help you reassess the relationship that you have with your dog.

Questions and Answers

Q *Hattie, my 10-month-old Bull Terrier has started growling at and mounting Molly, my three-year-old Bull Terrier. This behaviour started during her first season, which has just finished. She has always shared her food, bones, beds and everything with Molly. Now, when Molly is sitting on one side of me on the sofa and Hattie is on the other, Hattie will growl. Molly is very docile and submissive by nature, but I'm beginning to wish she would teach Hattie a lesson.*

A It is usual for bitches living in the same household to begin to compete with each other around season time. Nature has equipped them with a desire to pass on their genes to the next generation and it is important to them that they are the ones to have puppies at this time rather than their rivals. This makes them very competitive with other bitches in the household during seasons and accounts for Hattie's change in behaviour.

During her puppyhood, she may have found that Molly was gentle and submissive and no match for her in terms of pack leadership. As she matured and came into season, she could have tried to take her rightful place at the

▲ Strengths and weaknesses are discovered during play fighting, and this helps to establish a natural heirarchy between the two dogs.

top of the pack. I suspect that you try to treat both dogs equally, and this may be upsetting the fragile balance that now exists between them.

This may mean the dogs are okay with their roles until you interact with them. Then you probably accidentally reinforce Molly's status by petting her in equal amounts to Hattie. This effectively demotes Hattie which forces her to growl at Molly to try to retain her uncertain new role as leader. I suggest that you reinforce Hattie for a while, putting her first in everything, particularly giving her attention and affection first.

Push Mollie away from you when you are sitting on the sofa and make a fuss of Hattie (if you feel bad about this, give Hattie lots of fuss, then take Mollie out and give her all the attention she needs behind closed doors). You should try not to intervene too much in any of their squabbles, and don't shout or punish them as this raises the emotional temperature and may cause the dispute to escalate. Keep toys and bones out of the way until things have settled down.

It is a good idea to have both dogs spayed before their next seasons in order to prevent any further unrest during the next and subsequent seasons. Expect another three months or so of 'difficulty' between them while hormones settle down and they establish a proper pack order.

Neutering and its effects

Male and female puppies are born with different brains due to the effects of the different hormone levels to which they are exposed while they are still in their mother's womb.

In males at puberty, which occurs at about six months of age, the testes start producing testosterone, the male hormone. This causes changes in their brains and bodies that make them more likely to be successful at passing on their genes. These include physical changes, such as thicker skin and stronger muscles, and behaviour designed to pass on genes, such as interest in bitches in season, finding a mate, scent marking (frequent leg lifting, stronger smell), mounting and inter-male competition. If any of these behaviours are carried out to excess, they will usually become a problem both for the owners and the dog. Neutering can solve the problem provided that it is caused by circulating male hormones rather than by something else, such as fear or insecurity.

In females at puberty, the ovaries begin producing hormones that prepare the body for pregnancy. Seasons occur and the hormones that are produced at this time result in behaviour changes. Neutering can often help with the following problems:

▼ Male puppies are more likely to be exuberant and to play more competitively than females due to the effects of testosterone on their brains while in the womb.

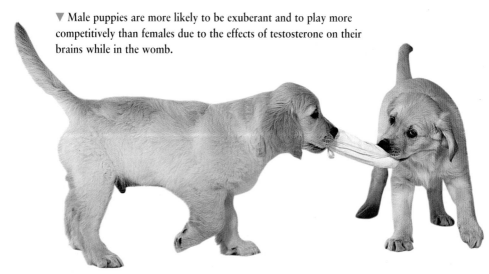

▶ Aggression between entire males is common in dogs that have not been allowed to learn how to settle competition disbutes amicably and especially those that always meet under restricted circumstances, such as on the lead.

■ Behaviour changes at season time, including escaping to find a mate.
■ Inter-female competition around and during season time, particularly between bitches that are kept together in the same family.
■ Behaviour changes during phantom pregnancies which occur after seasons, especially 'baby' guarding.

Is neutering the answer?

In dogs of either sex, neutering will not help with boisterousness, fear-related or status-related aggression and urine marking due to insecurity.

Fighting between entire males

Inter-male competition between entire dogs is normal. If both dogs are well socialized, they are unlikely to fight unless one of them will not back down. Usually, rituals and body posturing are enough to decide who will be top dog and gain access to bitches. If a dog is not well socialized and meets other entire dogs infrequently, it may begin to use aggression to gain the upper hand. If dogs meet regularly in the park, this quickly sets up a situation where they will fight on sight and their owners will have great difficulty keeping them apart.

Such territorial males will usually pass females, puppies and neutered males without a problem once they have checked them out, and may even play with them. Once territorial males have been neutered, the behaviour may continue for a while as some of the problem behaviour will be learnt. Additional behaviour therapy may be needed, especially in older dogs where the behaviour has been practised for a number of years.

Questions and Answers

Q My Cocker Spaniel, Toby is now five months old but, ever since we got him at eight weeks, we have seen some early signs of aggression and unwanted sexual behaviour as he will try to mount almost anything and then attack it. When we play with Toby with toys, he can become extremely aggressive. If you make eye contact with him, he will growl, snap and will occasionally bite. It is sometimes possible to calm him down by asking him to sit and calling him gently by his name, but his behaviour is very unpredictable. We are taking him to training classes and the teacher has suggested that, as Toby comes from trial-winning working stock, he may be frustrated by his position as a pet rather than a working dog. Do you have any suggestions as we don't know what to do for the best.

A It sounds as though Toby may not have had the best start in life. Many Cocker Spaniels are often bred for looks rather than their temperament and it can be very difficult for normal owners to rear them easily. The struggles you are having with Toby are not uncommon, but they are unnecessary if puppies come from stock that is bred for good temperaments. Dogs that are bred to be working dogs can be more difficult as they will have all the energy and persistence needed to win trials with an experienced owner. In addition, many puppies from working stock are kept outside in kennels and they are not adequately socialized or habituated for family life in a household.

I would suggest that you get some professional help now to sort out Toby's problems before they get any worse and he gets any older. By finding positive, non-aggressive ways to deal with the problems, you will be able to prevent his aggression developing.

Q *Harry is 14 months old and is not showing any signs of cocking his leg. He was neutered at six months. Can you suggest why?*

A Dogs that are neutered early in life sometimes never cock their legs. Leg cocking is not learned but induced by the surge of testosterone at puberty acting on the brain. It is a biological mechanism that enables male dogs to place their scent where rival males and receptive females can find it, i.e. at nose level. However, if dogs are neutered before the levels of hormone trigger this change in the brain, they do not cock their leg.

Dogs that are neutered early often retain a puppy-like appearance and fail to develop the other sexual characteristics of an entire male. This makes them easier to live with and there is no real need for a pet dog to cock his leg – in fact, it is slightly more convenient as, when out on a walk, they tend to stop less often to investigate and leave their own scent.

▲ Male puppies will not lift their leg to urinate until they have reached puberty.

CASE HISTORY

The fighting terrier family

Dogs: Jasmine, Yorkshire Terrier, five years, entire female; and
Poppy, Yorkshire Terrier, four years, entire female

Background

Five months ago, Jasmine gave birth to two female puppies, both of
which the owner decided to keep. A few weeks ago, Poppy came into
season and her owner took her to a stud dog to be mated. Since she came
into season, Poppy has been attacking the other dogs in the house.

Observations and diagnosis

The owner's house and garden were small and the floor was cluttered
with objects, reducing the space further. The owner had arthritis and
could not walk as far as the local park, but she did take the dogs out
regularly on leads. However, she was afraid to play with them in case
another fight broke out and, recently, Poppy had been given tablets to
keep her sedated. As is common in groups of females that are kept
together, both bitches came into oestrus at the same time. The puppies
had also recently reached sexual maturity and were in season.

Where resources are scarce and will only support one
litter of puppies, the top-ranking bitch of a pack will
be the one who has the puppies. If any puppies are
born to a lower-ranking bitch, they may be killed by
the top bitch so that her litter has a greater chance of
survival. Bitches in a pack will fight for the top spot
so that they have the right to pass on their genes to
the next generation. With the arrival of the new
puppies, resources in this household, particularly in
terms of space, were becoming
even more limited.
As Poppy was in
season, challenging
the other dogs to
win high status
had become
important to her.

Treatment plan

Since Poppy was now pregnant, it was important that she was not stressed as that stress would have been passed to her puppies, causing them to be more nervous, reactive, and difficult in later life. Giving her a separate area in which she could relax, where the others were not allowed, and where she could nest safely was suggested. This would reduce her need to challenge the others. The owner was given further advice on how to diffuse tension between the dogs, and spaying was recommended for all four bitches after seasons and pregnancies were over in order to prevent any further fighting.

Outcome

The owner created a nesting area for Poppy in an upstairs bedroom. She decided not to have her dogs spayed and, after consultation with her vet, agreed to put them all on medication to suppress their seasons until the puppies were old enough to be mated. Sadly, when the puppies were just three days old, and Poppy was taking a break in the garden, the owner forgot to shut the door to the bedroom and Jasmine got in with the litter and killed them all. The owner was devastated and she decided to give up breeding and eventually she had all the bitches spayed. After this, however, they settled down and they lived peacefully together.

Chapter 4

Aggression to other dogs

Aggression to other dogs is a very common behaviour problem. Many dogs are aggressive to others because of a lack of contact with other dogs which leads to fear and distrust. Others will have had traumatic experiences with some dogs that have attacked them. Some will have learned to play roughly with others and may bully them or 'attack' them through frustration when they are let off the lead. Aggression to other dogs can be a frightening and difficult problem for owners to manage. Care, time and patience are necessary for a successful resolution.

Fearful aggression

Puppies need to have lots of pleasant encounters with other dogs during the first 12 weeks of life if they are to get on well with them in later life. If they do not, they grow up wary and afraid of other dogs and are unable to read their intentions easily. Some breeds are more reactive than others, particularly herding breeds and terriers, and these dogs will need more and earlier socialization than others.

Another way for dogs to develop a fear of other dogs is through bad experiences. Many dogs are not good with others and it is quite easy for puppies to have frightening encounters with them, particularly if they are chased or bitten. Some dogs are too friendly and puppies can get a fright if they approach too fast or are too persistent.

▲ Puppies need to have plenty of pleasant encounters and play with other dogs while young if they are to grow up well socialised and unafraid of others.

Dogs commonly cope with fear in the following four ways:
- Freezing (keeping still and hoping that the threat goes away).
- Flight (running away).
- Fighting (scaring the other dog away or fighting).
- Appeasing (being silly and hoping it deters the other dog).

A dog will choose whichever strategy it thinks it will need to stay safe. Dogs rapidly learn that being held on a lead will prevent them from running away. Keeping still and appeasing often do not work and thus, for some dogs, being aggressive is the only option that is left open to them when the threat seems so severe.

This can be confusing for owners who assume that most dogs they meet are harmless, and can see no reason why their dog would not think so too. Since scared dogs usually produce an aggressive display, which is loud and explosive, and they do not look afraid when they do this, their owners can sometimes find it difficult to accept that fear is the reason behind this aggressive behaviour. In addition, some dogs are curious about other dogs and run up to them, only to find when they get there that they cannot cope and they decide they need to use aggression.

Aggression is more likely if the other dog approaches too quickly, if there is more than one dog, if the dogs meet in a restricted space, or if the owner is nervous and tightens the dog's lead.

▶ Puppies growing up in a family with other dogs will easily learn to read their body language. However, they also need socialisation with different types of dog if they are to be well adjusted in later life.

▶ A puppy needs to learn respect for older dogs so that it does not get too boisterous and out of control during play.

Solutions

As with all cases of aggression, it is important to get help from a good pet behaviour counsellor who will help you to reach a solution safely. Good use must be made of muzzles and long leads to prevent any injury or fright being caused to other dogs or their owners.

Finding other sociable dogs to work with is essential if you want to try to cure your dog. This is not easy and care needs to be taken not to stress the other dogs in the process. Alternatively, it is possible to teach your dog to focus on you while other dogs are around, keeping your distance at first and using games and food to maintain his attention. Gradually, as he learns to pay attention to you, you can slowly get closer to other dogs until he begins to prefer to concentrate on you than get involved with them.

◀ Relaxed, unguarded play is only possible if the participants trust each other.

Questions and Answers

Q *My terrier cross is a rescue dog. He is sometimes aggressive towards other dogs and pulls on his lead to get to them. What are the reasons behind this behaviour, and how can I correct it?*

A Terriers are renowned for being aggressive first and thinking later. If they are presented with what they see as a threat, they will readily go into 'attack' mode before thinking of other options, such as moving away or appeasement. So your dog puts up a good display to 'see the other dog off'. If he is aggressive to dogs to the point where he would bite or frighten them, seek help from a pet behaviour counsellor as this is not an easy problem to solve. They will teach you what to do when you see another dog coming and to focus your dog's attention on you instead. They will also help you to learn how to keep him feeling safe so that he sees you as a good leader who will take responsibility for getting rid of the threat. Then he can relax a little. They will also help you to introduce him to friendly dogs and increase his circle of friends if possible.

Q *My German Shepherd is 10 months old and quite aggressive towards other dogs (he was attacked by another dog when he was younger but he was scared of other dogs before this). Would neutering help or does he require proper training? I think most of his aggression stems from fear as he does most of the growling from behind me. If dogs get too close, however, he lunges towards them, barking and growling.*

A Neither neutering nor training will help. The answer lies in helping him overcome his fears by gradually desensitizing him and making happy associations with other dogs instead. He will need a structured plan of treatment to ensure that you make steady progress before he matures fully. You will need to find a good pet behaviour counsellor to help you so ask your veterinary surgeon for a recommendation. The pet behaviourist will help you to treat your dog's fear by teaching you how to gradually socialize him with other dogs and people, using food and toys to speed up the process while ensuring that no dogs or people get bitten or frightened. Until then, you can prevent him from getting any worse by accepting that he is frightened and not forcing him into situations that he cannot deal with. Good luck.

Frustrated play

Some dogs play a lot with other dogs when young, whether it's another dog in the family or on regular walks with other dogs. These dogs often do not spend much time playing with people. When the puppy grows up and finds that he cannot get to his friends to play as he is held on a lead, he becomes frustrated and this can result in aggression.

When on the lead, such dogs will be very excited and active, pulling, spinning and whining. They may play bow in the direction of other dogs and wag their tail furiously in greeting. However, eventually, this behaviour may be replaced by barking, growling and displays of aggression if the dog cannot get free. Sometimes this aggression is re-directed towards their owners and they may mouth or bite leads, or even people's legs or arms.

If a dog becomes very wound up in this way and is then left off the lead, he may go straight over to the other dog and become aggressive. If the other dog retaliates, then there may be a fight. If not, they will probably play once they have got to know each other, usually engaging in vigorous chase games.

This type of problem behaviour is common in dogs that have a high play or activity drive, particularly those that come from the working or herding breeds, and those with a strong character. Often these dogs have not learned to deal with frustrations in other areas of their life.

Solutions

1 You must teach your dog how rewarding it is to play with people. This may be difficult at first if he has spent all his life playing only with other dogs, but it is well worth you persevering.

2 You should also teach your dog how to deal with frustration in situations away from other dogs.

3 Once your dog is happy to play with people, you should teach him to play with you while other quiet dogs walk nearby.

4 Gradually work up until your dog will play with you while other dogs are running around off lead. Once he enjoys playing with people this much, he can be allowed to play with other dogs again. However, it is important to insist on good behaviour before letting him off lead.

◀ Dogs that are used to playing with other dogs will focus all their attention on them and may show intense unwanted behaviour in an attempt to get to them.

▼ Re-focusing their attention back onto their owner and teaching them how to play with humans is an important first step in solving the problem.

Predatory aggression

Some large dogs see small dogs running in the distance and mistake them for prey. This can lead to a chase and, if the large dog does not realize his mistake in time, to a predatory attack. Since the dog is trying to kill, serious damage can be inflicted. Once a dog is known to do this, he should be muzzled when he is outside and kept on a lead when small dogs are likely to be in the area. Since this problem is caused by an innate drive, there is no solution.

Questions and Answers

Q *We have an eight-year-old Staffie called Busby and a four-month-old Staffie puppy named Lucy who has been with us for six weeks. All is well apart from one problem: she will not stop nipping Busby. It is only in play and I'm sure she means no real harm, but nothing we do seems to help. I know that this is normal 'pack' behaviour and that, if left alone, dogs will find their own hierarchy but I find this increasingly difficult to do. Busby is mild mannered and although he occasionally gives a warning growl and then pushes Lucy away with his nose, she continues to nip and is drawing blood. He has puncture marks up his front legs and scabs from previous encounters.*

I've rung my vet and she says just leave them to it and perhaps put dressings on Busby's front legs as protection. We've tried this but, no matter what we do, the bandages slip off. I've started to put Lucy in a separate room (for a 'cooling off' period) when she nips him, in the hope that she will realize that her actions have consequences. When they are separated she becomes fretful and howls for him. Is this the correct thing to do? Will she realize that nipping him means she gets separated from him?

A Poor old Busby, I can just imagine how distressing it is for him when Lucy tugs away on the dressings on his legs or accidentally bites too hard. As she has only been with you for six weeks and is still a puppy, she will be very interested in playing with Busby as he plays in the same way as her littermates and speaks her language.

It is worth noting that the bull breeds inherit a higher pain threshold than other breeds of dog. This helps to explain why exploratory biting and mouthing by puppies is tolerated more readily by their thick-skinned mothers. Terriers also seem to play more roughly with their puppies than other types of dog. This, together with the fact that the bull breeds have strong jaw muscles, means that Staffie puppies tend to bite harder and to play more roughly than some other breeds.

Unfortunately for Busby, he is now the main source of play biting for Lucy, and it is not in his placid nature to curb her. Leaving them to it will be both unpleasant for Busby and will allow Lucy to learn all the wrong things about playing with other dogs. When she is older and tries to play with others in this rough way, they will probably react with aggression, eventually teaching her to be aggressive too in self defence.

To prevent this, practise your appropriately named 'cool off' periods more frequently in a more effective way. Attach a short line to Lucy's collar before she begins playing, and stop her when she becomes over-excited or does anything to Busby that unfamiliar dogs would find unacceptable. Lead her away from him and encourage her to play gentle games with firm rules with you instead. Do this every time she tries to play with Busby and she will soon learn that she cannot pester him, but can have a good time playing with you.

Keep play sessions to a minimum between them, and increase your play sessions with her, making sure they are short and packed with excitement. Use a stair gate to separate them at times when your attention is needed elsewhere. This will prevent Lucy practising rough games, without excluding her or denying her company – a better compromise than putting her in another room where it will be difficult for her to associate her isolation with her behaviour.

▲ Good use can be made of a stair gate to separate two dogs in the same household, allowing owners to teach the dogs to play games with them instead of each other.

Bullying

If a puppy grows up in a household where there is an older, weaker dog or a weaker sibling, he may acquire an inflated idea of his own capabilities. If the older dog or other puppy allows the puppy to jump on them, play whenever he wants, and really sink his teeth in without telling him off, the puppy may learn to play in this way and enjoy it.

This may also happen if the puppy is taken to socialization classes and allowed to play for a long time in an uncontrolled way. As the puppy grows up, he will learn to enjoy increasingly rough and controlling games.

However, when the puppy reaches adolescence and he tries to play similar games with other dogs, he is likely to find that they will not tolerate this behaviour and that they will become aggressive. Such encounters quickly teach the bullying puppy to get in there first to make sure he overpowers his opponent more quickly.

When the bullying dog is on the lead and sees another dog, he will keep still, give direct eye contact and assume a confident posture with a

▶ Allowing dogs to bully others in play can lead to trouble when they meet another dog that is not so tolerant.

stiff tail with the tip wagging. Off lead, however, he will go straight up to the other dog, sometimes flying straight into aggression or a shoulder charge. Some dogs will strut and try to intimidate, giving strong eye contact and placing their paws on the back of the other dog. If there is no obvious submission from the other dog, then there may be an attack.

Strong-willed dogs with a high play or activity drive are most likely to develop this problem, particularly if they have not met many dogs other than the ones with whom they have grown up. The bull breeds, with their bodies that are relatively insensitive to pain, are also more likely to develop this problem.

Solutions

It is difficult to turn very aggressive bullying dogs around, and help should be sought from an experienced pet behaviour counsellor. Until then, the dog should be kept on a lead and exercised in a safe area away from other dogs. The solution lies in teaching the dog to enjoy playing vigorous but gentle games with humans rather than other dogs. This is not easy as the dog will often get great enjoyment from bullying others and playing rough games, which will have to be matched in excitement by relatively gentle games with humans. For some aggressive dogs, particularly if they are large and likely to cause injury, it may be necessary to stop all further contact with other dogs for the rest of their life.

▶ Confident dogs that have learnt to bully others will often watch for signs of submission in the other dog before deciding whether to attack or play.

Questions and Answers

Q *Wilson is a Border Collie/German Shepherd cross whom we acquired from the local RSPCA rescue centre last year. He has been the perfect dog except for one thing. If we take him to a playing field or a park and he sees another dog when he is off the lead, he will run as fast as he can up to the dog and almost brush past, barking aggressively for a few moments. When he has managed to stop, he will run back to the dog, barking and acting aggressively, and then suddenly stop and ignore the dog.*

Sometimes Wilson will end up playfully chasing the dog and they may play together as if they have been friends for years. He tries to respond to our commands, but eventually the draw of the other dog becomes so strong that no amount of calling will prevent him from approaching the dog. He has never actually attacked another dog, and will even run away if the other dog acts aggressively towards him. He has been neutered and is perfect with people and dogs he knows. What can we do about this?

▲ Dogs that play rough games are at risk of retaliatory aggression themselves which then causes them to become defensive, thereby exacerbating the problem.

▲ Teaching rough players to focus on games with their owners helps to prevent them getting involved with other dogs and causing trouble.

A This type of behaviour is often the result of learning to play roughly with another dog or puppy when young. Later, when they are old enough to go out, such dogs try to play these inappropriate games with other dogs which will result in aggression from other dogs who will not tolerate such behaviour. Once this has happened, although they would like to play with other dogs, they are not sure of their reception and develop a strategy to try to work out if the other dog is friendly while protecting themselves in case they are not.

It is very difficult for you to cure your dog as he has already learned that some dogs are not friendly. The best way is to teach him to play with toys and then make games with toys so exciting that he would rather play with you than run up to other dogs. This is not always easy to do since he will have spent a long time playing with other dogs. However, it will give good results if you are able to do so. To be really effective, you probably need to stop him playing with other dogs for six months so that he learns that all his games come from you now.

The other alternative is to put Wilson on a lead whenever you see other dogs unless you know that the dog is friendly and can take his 'over the top' approach. If all the dogs he meets are nice to him, he may begin to give up his unusual approach gradually, but it will take quite a while.

CASE HISTORY

Aggression to other dogs

Dogs: Harry, seven months, Border Collie, entire male; and Frank, three years, terrier cross, entire male

Background

Harry came from a farm when he was 12 weeks old. He lived with a terrier cross called Frank who was known to be aggressive occasionally to other dogs. Harry had started getting into a frenzy and biting Frank when he saw another dog. Since taking him out for walks alone, he had bitten his owner twice on her legs when he saw another dog.

Observations and diagnosis

The owners lived on a very hostile housing estate where both people and dogs were unfriendly. During a short walk to the local park, at least five dogs rushed to their gates as we passed, barking ferociously

and giving us quite a scare. Harry's owner was reactive, very nervous and unsure of what to do when Harry behaved in this way. When let off the lead in the park, Harry was a totally different dog, running after his toy and playing with the other dogs he encountered. When Frank was taken out, he was fine with other dogs unless they started to behave aggressively, at which point he became immediately aggressive and would not back down.

Harry grew up on a farm and did not encounter other dogs until he was already at the end of his critical socialization period. He then went to live with a dog who taught him to be aggressive when other dogs acted aggressively and an owner who added to his fears by being nervous herself. Being bred from generations of reactive Collies, he soon learned to get ready for action when taken out on the housing estate. Due to his state of high arousal during these encounters, and with no outlet for all his energy and excitement, he reverted to his favourite game – biting Frank. When this option was removed, he bit the next best thing instead.

Treatment plan

Harry was muzzled while he was walking through the estate in order to prevent any injury to Frank or his owner, or these walks were avoided entirely if it was possible. The owner was also advised to avoid walking past any dogs that rushed out to bark at their gates, even if this meant crossing the road several times in order to get to the park or, better still, taking the dogs to the park in the car.

When aggressive incidents occurred, the owner was to take control of the situation, putting herself between the dogs and the aggressor's gate, and then moving away so that her dogs learned that they could rely on her to sort out the problem, leaving them free to relax. It was decided also that Harry should be taught to focus his attention onto a toy when other dogs were present. A programme of teaching Harry to do this while other dogs got progressively nearer while he was on the lead was carefully implemented by the owner.

Outcome

Two months later the owner wrote to say that Harry was now making steady progress. He had learned to respond to her 'what's this?' cue with his full attention and she could use this with the promise of a game with a toy to get him to pass all but the most aggressive of dogs.

Chapter 5

Puppy problems

Puppies take time to learn human ways and do not come with an in-built programme of how to behave in the human world. They need to be taught what to do and educated well to enable them to behave well. It is normal to experience some behaviour problems as they grow up. Luckily, these are usually easy to solve as they will not have developed into ingrained bad habits. If you do the right thing, puppy problems can usually be sorted out within a month and it should not take more than a few days to see an improvement.

Play biting

Puppies play with each other by wrestling, chasing and biting. When they are separated from their littermates and taken to a human household, they will try to play with us in the same way. This makes it likely that they will bite at our hands, faces, hair, feet and clothing.

This is an exciting game for them, especially since their milk teeth are very sharp and we often squeal and pull away, making us more fun to run after. As a puppy grows, the bites become increasingly painful and, if uncontrolled, an adult dog with this problem can cause severe bruising, even though his intention is only to play. Children are often play-bitten as they are fast moving with exciting, high-pitched voices which will encourage the puppy to play, chase and grab them.

Some puppies are likely to play bite more than others. Terriers tend to play rough naturally with their littermates and mothers. By the time they arrive at their new home, they have already learnt to bite hard in play. Some puppies of the bull breeds also bite harder than others because they have much larger, broader heads, giving

◀ Play biting is a natural, important part of puppy play. Young puppies need to learn to play with toys when they play with humans instead.

them stronger jaws. These dogs are also likely to be relatively insensitive to pain, making it easier for them to play rough and not to feel the bites of the other puppy. Some owners encourage puppies to play rough and tumble games, allowing the puppy to bite their hands and to hang on to their clothing. Puppies that have high energy levels and a limited outlet for that energy are also more likely to develop this problem.

Solutions

Since your puppy is trying to get you to play, it is important to have a toy ready whenever you interact with him. Keep your hands and everything

▲ When a puppy play bites, try to keep as still as possible so that he learns that there is no excitement or enjoyment to be found in biting humans.

else still, and the toy moving. Try to ignore the bites and encourage the puppy away from your hands with the toy. If the bites are too persistent or too hard, yelp loudly enough to stop him in his tracks, then offer the moving toy instead. If this does not stop the puppy, you should get up, walk away and end the game every time he bites too hard, or use a line to stop him reaching human skin, putting only the toy within range.

Make sure that the toy playing is both fun and rewarding for the dog. It has to be more fun than biting owners. Provide many of these play sessions throughout the day so that the puppy learns appropriate ways to play and he no longer needs to play inappropriately.

◀ Wriggle the toy and keep it moving so that the puppy will be attracted to it and encouraged to play and bite on it instead.

Questions and Answers

Q *Do you have any advice on how to curb a three-month-old Labrador's desire to snap and attack clothes and ankles?*

A At three months, this is likely to be just excited play when he is presented with something exciting to chase and grab as people move around him. To begin with, make sure that he is getting plenty of exciting play sessions throughout the day by keeping soft toys around the house so that you can play with him frequently. Keep these sessions short and make them fun and full of excitement and movement. This should provide him with an outlet for his energies and make it less likely that he will try to get a game with people when they walk past him.

Leave a short line attached to his collar when you are in the house with him and use this to stop him giving chase or grabbing at clothes and ankles at other times. When there are lots of people around or excited children, you should make use of a stair gate or a puppy playpen to restrict his activities and teach him to remain quiet and calm when he is faced with exciting opportunities.

▶ Although not acceptable, it is a natural reaction for puppies to run after and bite at moving objects, including the clothing of humans in their family.

Q Whenever we come in from work, in spite of the fact that she is not left alone during the day, Millie has started to bite either my or my husband's elbows and back. Her tail wags and she barks excitedly, but this is becoming annoying and painful! She doesn't respond to a firm 'no' although she does at other times. When put onto the floor she persists in jumping up again. This lasts from five minutes to half an hour and then she flops and wants a fuss. Where am I going wrong?

A It sounds like Millie is just playing but in an inappropriate way for a pet dog. Young puppies often try to get us to play as they used to do with their littermates by nipping and barking excitedly. Even though you get cross and try to stop her, you are still reacting, and, for her, this is much more rewarding than being ignored.

▲ Moving feet are an easy target for excited, playful puppies.

When you get in, greet her warmly for a few seconds, holding her collar if necessary to ensure good behaviour, then ignore her completely, turning your back and walking away slowly if she tries to instigate a play fight. Only pay attention to her when she is calm and quiet and you are ready. In addition, you need to develop planned play sessions set aside specifically to use some of that puppy exuberance. Initiate games yourself and play often, and she will soon be waiting patiently for the next session rather than trying to start her own by showing unwanted behaviour.

Dealing with frustration

Dogs that have always had their own way and have not learnt to deal with frustration can sometimes behave badly when they are prevented from having or doing something, such as the freedom to go where they please or attention from their owner. They are focused on the thing that they want and become very excited, sometimes barking, growling, nipping or biting at anything around them in their frustration.

A good example of this type of behaviour is when a dog who has never been held still before is restrained. He may start throwing himself around, struggling and wriggling to loosen the grip, and he may even bite at the hands of the person who is holding him in order to free himself.

Dogs that live in a human world need to learn to live with the feelings that are provoked when they cannot get their own way, and it is always easiest if this is done while they are still young before they grow up and their bodies get bigger and stronger, thereby making it even harder for their owners to keep controlling them. This sort of problem behaviour is particularly common among strong-willed dogs, especially if they are owned by gentle, easy-going people or by inexperienced owners who have never had a dog before.

Solutions

In order to solve this problem, it is necessary for you to set up some situations where your dog experiences mild frustration and, when he has calmed down, he is allowed to get what he wants. You should not react, no matter what your dog does, so this may mean using a chain lead so that your dog cannot chew through it, and tying him up somewhere where he cannot do any damage or cause a nuisance by barking.

You should offer your dog something that he really wants, such as food or a toy, and place it just out of his reach. You must ignore any unwanted behaviour. If he tries to get your attention, do not speak, look or touch him until he stops. You may find that his behaviour gets worse before it gets better as he will try harder to get what he wants. However, you must wait until he is completely calm before releasing him to get what he wants or paying him attention.

You must carry this out several times a day until your dog no longer shows the unwanted behaviour. Then it will be necesssary to find other places to do this and repeat the process. Once he is calm in these situations, you should go back to the place where you first experienced the problem and teach your dog how to behave well in the same way, i.e., by waiting until he is calm before letting him free to enjoy the reward that you are offering in return for his good behaviour.

▲ With your dog on a lead, tease him with something he would like, such as an interesting toy or a tasty treat.

◀ Once the reward has been thrown a short distance away, restrain your dog so that he cannot go to it. When he has calmed down and has accepted the restraint, set him free to get his reward.

Questions and Answers

Q *I have an eight-month-old Springer Spaniel. When we are out for a walk she is very excitable and starts barking furiously at me when I stop for any reason, i.e. sit on a bench, talk to someone or stop for my son to play on the swings. This is my second Springer who has behaved like this, so I realize it is my fault but would like some tips on how to cure this problem. She is very good at retrieving but I stopped throwing the ball for her after this problem started because I feel it is aggravating the situation. What should I do?*

A Your dog knows that she can get you to move on by barking and this is why she does it. You will need to find a place in the park or at home where barking does not matter. Take her toys with you and keep them hidden. Walk to the chosen place, stop or sit down, and ignore any barking. Ignoring means not touching her, looking at her or speaking to her. Turn away from her, take some ear plugs if you need to, but keep ignoring her until she is quiet, even if it takes a very long time at first.

For interest, count how many times she barks. When she is quiet, count to three, then quickly take her toy out of your pocket and throw it. Repeat as many times as you can on the walk. You will notice that the barking gets worse for a while as she tries harder to get you to respond. Then there will be a dramatic decrease in the barking. When she is quiet when you stand still, throw her toy immediately. It may take a while to achieve this but it will be worth persevering.

When your dog is quiet in those areas where barking does not matter, you should take her to places where it does and then repeat the process. Hang on for quiet, try not to get tense and then reward her with a run in the same way. At other times, you should never let her off the lead until she is quiet and always wait for quiet before leaving the house or moving forward when she is on the lead. If she barks at any time, deliberately stand still and then wait for three seconds of quiet before moving on again.

It is important to be consistent and to try not to lapse back into your old habits when someone stops to speak to you. Practise meeting your friends until both of you know how to behave well! Gradually your dog will learn that barking at you is not worthwhile and she will give up.

Housetraining problems

As soon as they are able to, puppies instinctively move out of the nest to go to the toilet. If they are raised in clean conditions, it is possible to housetrain them in a few days if you are vigilant. However, you will need to concentrate as young puppies have baby brains and bodies and therefore they cannot hold on for too long.

Puppies need to be taken out after waking up or resting, after eating, after playing or any excitement and at least every two hours. You always need to go out with the puppy, not shut him out alone. Eliminatory behaviour is self-rewarding, but it may help to praise and give treats for going in the right place. Watch out for any tell-tale signs that your puppy wants to go when he is in the house and take him out at once.

If you have to go out or cannot concentrate on your puppy, then leave him in a play pen that has a bed and a toilet area. The toilet area should be covered with polythene and newspaper. At night-time, you can either take your puppy up to your bedroom with you and confine him to a small area, getting up to take him out when he wakes, or leave him downstairs in a puppy playpen, getting up to take him out when you hear him make a noise.

Housetraining tips
- If you fail to go outside with your puppy, he will try to get back inside the house and will still need to go once he does, so always accompany him.
- Do not pick up the puppy whenever he attempts to go in the house. If you do so, he will not learn to go to the door to be let out.
- Do not punish the puppy whenever you see him going inside the house. If you do so, he will learn to hide away, making it more difficult to housetrain him.
- Do not leave the puppy alone for too long. He will learn to go on the surface on which he has been left and will think that the carpet, tiles or newspaper is his toilet.

Questions and Answers

Q *My dog Honey is a seventeen-week-old bitch German Shepherd puppy. She is generally clean in most of the house, even where she sleeps during the night. She will, however, persist in urinating both just outside and in my wife's bedroom. Is there any way of stopping this habit?*

A Clean the areas thoroughly so the smell is not attracting her back to the same spot. Use a warm biological washing powder solution; allow to dry and rub over with surgical spirit. Place large items over the marked areas for a few days to break the habit. If she chooses another spot near to or in your wife's bedroom, she may be marking her territory rather than just needing to go to the toilet (territory marking usually involves small amounts of urine whereas toileting usually produces lots). If this is the case, look for signs of insecurity. Consider the times she urinates to see if there is a pattern, e.g. when visitors arrive or she is left. If insecurity is the problem, treating the cause is the solution.

Q *How can I stop my Boxer puppy soiling in the house at night? She spends a lot of time outside during the day, and we always take her out late to go to the toilet. We do not feed her after 6.30 pm, but she has always soiled when we go down in the morning. Please help.*

A Some puppies take longer to learn to be clean at night than others; you should not expect puppies under six months to hold on all night. Take her with her bed to your room and tie her so that she cannot get out of bed. If you don't want her in the bedroom, put her within hearing range, leaving the door open. Take care how you tie her; don't use a check-chain. Ignore her after saying goodnight; if she wakes up, wait a few moments and take her into the garden. Wait with her until she does something, then praise her and take her back to bed. As she has to wait until she is taken out, she will grow out of the habit and, after being clean for two weeks, can be returned to the kitchen.

Submissive urination

This is a natural behaviour where a puppy produces a small amount of urine when being greeted by an animal with a perceived higher rank. Humans often punish this behaviour, mistaking it for proper urination, and this usually makes the problem even worse or it may continue into adulthood.

Solutions

In order to tackle this, the puppy's confidence needs to be boosted by using reward-based training rather than rebukes for bad behaviour. Until then, greetings should be kept low key and done outside or on a surface that can be soiled without a problem.

▲ Showing submission is a natural behaviour for puppies when they are faced with a bigger, more confident dog. Producing a small amount of urine will help the puppy to tell the older dog that he is no threat.

Adolescent problems

During the first six months, puppies are very dependent on their owners for the care needed to survive. As a consequence, they spend a lot of time building a strong relationship with their owners. This is very rewarding for owners who usually enjoy the puppy's attention and responsiveness.

When a puppy reaches puberty at around six months, his body becomes bigger, stronger, more energetic and his confidence grows. Just like normal adolescent children, his focus of attention naturally shifts from his owners and home to the outside world. This can be difficult for the owners to accept as, suddenly, their attentive, well-behaved puppy has been replaced by a gangly adolescent who is not really interested in them any more.

Since hormone levels change dramatically at puberty, the behaviour of puppies changes accordingly. They become more interested in other dogs and in scents around their territory. Sometimes, there is a temporary breakdown in housetraining, particularly as bitches come into season for the first time, even in dogs that have previously been very clean.

In addition to this, with their increased confidence, some puppies may decide to test the boundaries and challenge their owners if the owners

▲ As their attention turns away from their owner to the wider world, adolescent dogs may begin to ignore their owner and become less responsive to requests.

have not made it clear that they are in charge. For puppies with existing behaviour problems, their extra confidence makes it more likely that they will deal with things in a more forceful way, perhaps using aggression to see off any threats rather than choosing to run away.

Solutions

During adolescence, it is important that you keep control in order to prevent your dog running off, escaping and getting lost. It is natural for him to want to explore the world outside without you, and this may lead to him not coming back when you call. Use a long line (be careful not to get tangled in it) or exercise him in a secure area if necessary. Make sure that your garden fences are secure.

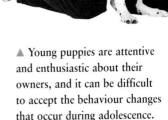

▲ Young puppies are attentive and enthusiastic about their owners, and it can be difficult to accept the behaviour changes that occur during adolescence.

Continue with your training programme, channeling your puppy's energy into learning, working, exercising and playing games with you. This will help him to enjoy being with you rather than in the outside world, and you may be able to hold his attention for longer periods if you keep the training sessions short and fun.

Be realistic about your expectations during this period and bear in mind that this stage will soon pass. Once your dog has begun to reach maturity (at approximately one to two years old), you will find that he settles down again and will become the dog that you always wanted after all.

▲ Keep adolescent dogs focused on you as much as possible and remember that their adolescence does not last for ever.

Questions and Answers

Q *Our seven-month-old puppy keeps pulling out and destroying plants in our garden. He used to dig in the flower beds when he was little, but we didn't mind this as he didn't make much mess. However, now that he is older, he pulls up shrubs and is also trying to dig under the fences. We are worried that he may get out one day. How can we stop this behaviour?*

A It is quite natural for a seven-month-old puppy to go off exploring his environment and venturing further from home. As you have to keep your puppy within the confines of the garden, he is finding things to do to use up his energy and desire to explore. To stop him destroying the plants, you will need to give him something else to do. What will work depends on what sort of dog he is and what he enjoys. If he likes to

▲ Terriers love to dig and their need for exploration is at its peak during adolescence. In addition, their bodies are stronger and they have more energy than when they were smaller. Owners should provide plenty of alternative activities as the key to getting through this problematic time.

chew, give him objects that will take him a long time to deal with such as large strong toys that have been stuffed with cream cheese or meat paste. Rawhide chews are usually dealt with quickly, so buy large ones and hide them inside a cardboard box so he has to work out how to get to them. Large, raw meaty marrow bones will keep him busy for a while, but do make sure that he does not eat too much of the bone at once.

Give your dog a special digging area and teach him to find items that you have buried there on a regular basis. Suspend some toys from trees and tuck small bits of treat inside them to get him interacting with them (be careful that he cannot harm himself when doing this). If he eats dry food, then try feeding his dinner inside a special ball that only lets the food out slowly as he rolls it around.

You will need to keep an eye on him to check that he is not doing anything he shouldn't, but if you give him plenty of new and interesting things to do, he should prefer to do those instead. This is very important when he digs near to fences as, at his age, he will have a strong desire to get out and run off to explore. You may like to place some sheets of wire netting down under the fence in those areas where he is most persistent so that he cannot tunnel out.

Make sure that he has plenty of exercise by taking him out for long walks every day. You should try to take him to new places regularly so that he can explore. Fortunately, dogs do not stay in the adolescent stage for ever and in about another three months or so, he should have calmed down!

CASE HISTORY

Second dog problems

Dog: Benji, Boxer, eight months, entire male; and Jack, Boxer, eight years, entire male

Background

Benji grew up with Jack. Their owners were pleased that they played well together as they had wanted a companion and friend for Jack and it seemed to have given him a new lease of life. It also meant that they did not have to take either dog for walks as they played together energetically during the day and were too tired by the evening.

However, when Benji reached adolescence, the owners noticed that he was not as lovable as Jack, even though they had taken care to go back to the same breeder. Benji was more disobedient; he would run after other dogs in the park; and he did not enjoy being fussed over or petted as Jack did.

Observations

When Benji was separated and then brought back to Jack and his owners, he greeted Jack first, taking no notice of his owners. If the owners called Benji, he would wait until Jack, encouraged by the calling, got up to go to them. Then he would run over to Jack, licking his face and getting very excited, accidentally going towards the owners in the process. Jack obviously preferred his owners to Benji, but Benji preferred Jack to his owners. In the park, Benji would run off to play with other dogs and no amount of calling could make him return. Eventually, the owners of the dogs with whom he was playing took them home and Benji would return to see what Jack was doing.

Treatment plan

A treatment plan was devised specifically with the purpose of separating Benji from Jack when they were left alone by the owners. If Benji was to build a good relationship with his owners, then he needed to stop getting all his social contact and play from Jack. This meant that they would have to be separated for a while to stop them playing together when the owners were not there to supervise them. When the owners were there, however, Jack and Benji could be together, but all play between them must be interrupted and stopped.

Change the relationship

The owners needed to work hard at teaching Benji to play with them. This would be difficult at first, but it would have to be continued until he enjoyed playing with the owners as much or more than he enjoyed playing with Jack. Only then could he be allowed to go back to playing with Jack. Benji should also spend more time with his owners. He should go out on walks and outings with them only so that he could learn to be dependent on them rather than on Jack.

Outcome

After many months of hard work, Benji became more responsive to his owners, going to them for attention and sometimes dropping things in their lap for them to throw. He started enjoying playing human games and his recall improved as he learned that it would be fun to return to his owners and then be let free again.

▲ A young dog growing up in a two-dog household can become isolated from its owners as it gets all the social contact it needs from the other dog.

Chapter 6

Hierarchy issues

In the wild, dogs live in a hierarchy where the individuals are ranked according to status. While the desire to reach the top of the hierarchy is very much watered down in most pet dogs, there are still some for whom being of high status is very important. Although this is rare, there are some individuals who compete with others living in the household to reach the 'top dog' position. Status-related aggression is easily confused with fear aggression, and great care should be taken to get an accurate diagnosis before beginning treatment.

Status problems

Wolves, the ancestors of our domestic pet dogs today, live in packs and arrange themselves into a hierarchy structure with the high-status individuals at the top and those that are low-ranking at the bottom.

However, the order is not fixed and will change as circumstances and the fitness of the individuals change. The hierarchy is built and maintained by a complex set of competitions, encounters, body language signals and actions so that each individual learns and keeps to its place in the pack. The function of the hierarchy is to reduce the amount of fighting over resources, particularly at feeding time when lethal competition could otherwise take place. The hierarchy ensures that the resources go to the strongest individuals first. These are the ones that stand the best chance of survival, and hence will go on to produce the next generation if resources are scarce.

In domestic dogs, the genes that lead to a desire to be top of the hierarchy have been watered down drastically. However, for some ambitious dogs, gaining the upper hand in relationships and taking

◀ Losing every game of tug-of-war can encourage your dog to think that he is stronger than you and better able to lead the pack.

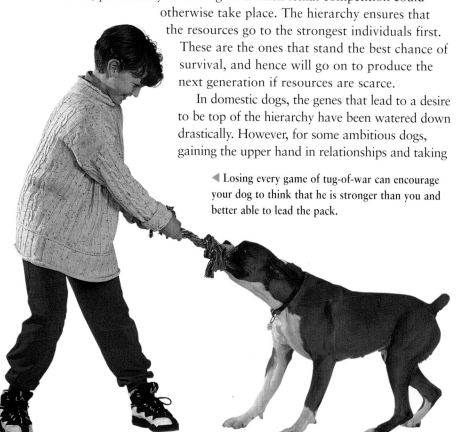

▲ Sofas are a valued resource and some high-ranking dogs will challenge owners from here. However, more commonly, dogs are worried about being told off when on the sofa and are aggressive to their owners through fear.

control is still important. The number of dogs that are like this is very small, but, occasionally, some dogs will take advantage of a kind owner. This is particularly likely in strong-willed breeds, such as Cocker Spaniels, Westies, Soft-Coated Wheaten Terriers and the guarding breeds. These dogs may begin to challenge their owners as they mature during adolescence. If they are successful, they will become more and more controlling, resorting to biting if necessary in an effort to get their own way. These dogs are generally very friendly to strangers as well as their owners, but their behaviour can change dramatically when they do not get what they want.

Solutions

The relationship between the dog and his owners needs to be carefully changed to shift the balance of power back to the owners. This cannot be done by force and owners need to gradually begin winning all encounters that they were previously losing. This may be over things of which they were unaware; for example, they may always have given toys back to their dog at the end of the play session as they did not want them. This encourages the dog to think that he is stronger and more able as he is always able to get toys from them during competitions. If he is already aggressive, specialist help is needed to put the owners back on top safely and successfully.

Questions and Answers

Q *My Samoyed dog gets very protective over my kitchen and bedroom, and he barks at me whenever I go into either room. He does not do this to anyone else. What should I do?*

A It could be a sign of dominant behaviour as controlling movements of the pack around the territory is a good way for a dog to raise his status if he wishes to become the leader. You do not say how old he is or whether he is prepared to do anything other than barking if you take no notice. I suggest you get professional help, especially if your dog is an adolescent or young adult and he is difficult to groom, disobedient or controlling in other ways. Although this is not a major problem at the moment, your dog could decide to escalate his aggression over encounters he is not winning and could become confident enough to bite eventually. Alternatively, he could be just excited that you are moving and may need more exercise and things to do! A pet behaviour counsellor will help you to sort this out and tell you whether or not there is any cause for concern.

Q *I have a seven-month-old Lhasa Apso. Occasionally she growls and snaps at me when she does not want to do something, i.e. when told to get off the sofa or when I pick her up to put her to bed. Yesterday, when I tried to wipe her face after her meal, she bit me quite badly. When she growls or tries to bite, what should I do?*

A It is likely that, at seven months, your dog is challenging you for the top dog position in your household. If you have had her from a puppy, she will have been watching and taking note of all the encounters you have had. Now she has enough confidence to begin throwing out small challenges (probably when you try to get her to do something she doesn't want to do, such as going to her bed at night). If she wins these or notices that you only just win, her challenges will increase. What you need is expert help so that you can see where, in her eyes, you have been going wrong and she can begin to see you as a strong pack leader rather than a weak one. Shouting and smacking are not the answer, but finding out how top dogs keep control of their pack without resorting to violence is. Alternatively, she could be worried about your intentions and has only just developed enough confidence to try to keep you away.

CASE HISTORY

Status-related aggression

Dog: Pepe, Long-haired Dachshund, five years, neutered male

Background

Pepe's owner was elderly and found it easy to let Pepe decide when things should happen, such as when to eat and when to go for a walk. Gradually, Pepe began to get his way in all areas of life and looked upon it as his right to have just what he wanted when he wanted it. He also began to take on the responsibility for looking after his owner and, if he didn't like visitors, he barked and made such a fuss that his owner eventually had to ask them to leave. Pepe's owner enjoyed this relationship as she felt protected.

▲ Pepe makes it clear that he does not want to be picked up at this time and requests that his owner put him back down on the floor immediately.

Things changed as Pepe's owner began to get older and became more frail. Pepe had long since become cross when his owner paid all her attention to the handset instead of him when she answered the phone. He would bite at the legs of the table on which the phone stood until, eventually, his owner had had to stand it in tin cans to prevent the legs being destroyed. From this, he moved on to barking so loudly that his owner could not hear what was being said on the other end of the telephone. Due to a series of health problems, Pepe's owner became increasingly reliant on the phone to call for help and eventually her health advisors suggested she get rid of Pepe in case he prevented her from doing this.

Observations and diagnosis

Pepe was totally in control of his elderly owner. If he wanted to be picked up, he jumped up and down in front of her until she did so. If she picked him up when he didn't want to be held, he would growl and show his teeth so that she put him down again. He dictated where she went and what she did. If she tried to get him to do things that he did not want to do, such as getting off the sofa, he threatened aggression and she quickly gave up. He slept on her bed at night and growled if she turned over, but she felt protected and less alone if he was there.

Treatment plan

A slow reduction in Pepe's privileges was implemented. His owner took control of the feeding times at first, keeping to a set routine and ignoring his demands for food at other times. She gave him affection when he was behaving well and ignored him when he was not. She used a house-line to move him off the sofa and into different areas of the house when she wanted him to be elsewhere, especially when she wanted to answer the telephone.

Outcome

Pepe reluctantly accepted these changes and his behaviour changed sufficiently for him to allow his owner to use the telephone in peace. He became less demanding and more playful, allowing his owner to groom him and to shut him outside if a visitor came to the house.

▲ Pepe, before treatment, scratching at the carpet around the legs of the telephone table in frustration when his owner answered a call.

Hierarchy problems between dogs

In a stable dog pack, there is a big difference in status between individuals. If they are similar in status, the underdog may challenge for supremacy and fighting can occur. Pack stability is helped if there is no shortage of resources.

The function of hierarchy is to ensure that top dogs have automatic right of access to important resources in times of shortage. The right to breed is one of the privileges of high status and it is important to individuals. Seasons accentuate any problems that may already exist in the hierarchy, and fighting between bitches can be severe. Dogs are born with different amounts of ambition, which, as they grow up, is accentuated or diminished by the environment. Dogs that win games and encounters have different expectations to those that always lose; they are likely to be more confident with a stronger desire to win. Physical ability can increase their chances of winning encounters, but mental strength is often more important.

If pet dogs don't fight when left alone, the weaker dog probably knows its place and does not dare challenge, suggesting that the owner is influencing the situation and may be causing the problem. If owners try to treat dogs equally, it raises the status of the underdog and lowers that of the top dog. This gives the underdog ideas above his station and he challenges, causing the top dog to fight harder to keep control.

Solutions

Find out what the natural hierarchy would be if there were no outside influences. Which dog naturally has most access to territory, chews, food, games and attention? Which dog moves away so the other dog can get to the bed or through a doorway? If there is a natural hierarchy, make sure there are enough resources and treat the top dog preferentially. This does not mean denying the underdog but simply providing good things for the top dog first, such as food, games and affection. If the dogs already fight, seek professional help to reach a safe, successful solution. Alternatively, dogs may fight only when a bitch is in season nearby; bitches may fight only during seasons. Having these dogs neutered helps solve the problem.

CASE HISTORY

Fighting in the family

Dogs: Frieda, Lurcher, seven years, neutered female; and Greta, Whippet, nine years, neutered female

Background

The owner is a veterinary nurse and the dogs were acquired as adults. Frieda was left at the surgery with a broken leg. Greta belonged to a child until the novelty wore off and was then kept in a small kennel for years with little human contact. After the dogs had lived together for a year, Frieda attacked Greta who needed extensive stitching. Eighteen months later, Greta was

being petted by a visitor and Frieda attacked again, causing a wound that needed stitches. Another 18 months passed and Greta got under the feet of a horse, panicked and started yelping. This triggered an instant savage attack from Frieda round the throat. She has never shown any aggression to the owner's other dogs.

If Frieda attacked, it was with considerable force, and Greta did not retaliate. This was consistent with Frieda having never learned to inhibit her bite by playing with people and other dogs. The owner was knowledgeable,

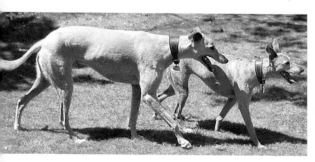

sensible and caring; a firm pack leader who did not tolerate disagreements between the dogs. Frieda had a dull coat and a worried expression as if weighed down by the responsibility of maintaining her status. Greta pestered

her, biting at her face and posturing with tail up and body pushes. The owner prevented Frieda from putting a stop to this behaviour by inhibiting her aggressive responses and was, therefore, unwittingly altering the natural balance between them. Greta accepted Frieda's high status when they were alone as there was no fighting when the owner was out.

Treatment plan

Given the severity of the injuries inflicted, it was inadvisable to leave the two dogs alone together without supervision. The plan involved stopping Greta 'hounding' Frieda and teaching her to play so Frieda could relax and become less resentful. She was given a daily time-out period when she could give up the responsibilities of being higher in status to Greta. It was important that Frieda's thoughtful and intelligent sensitivities were appreciated and she was not 'put down' in front of Greta by being shouted at, told off or touched roughly. She was put first, e.g. when getting into the car, feeding and going through doorways. The owner talked softly and touched her gently to help her relax. Reducing her stress levels was important since high stress would lower her threshold of aggression and make 'losing her temper' with Greta over small incidents more likely.

Outcome

Frieda is a lot more relaxed, seems happier with life and her coat has begun to shine. Greta no longer pesters her, is more respectful to her and accepts her place below Frieda in the pack, even when the owner is present.

Chapter 7

Chasing concerns

Some dogs chase because they enjoy it, while others chase away things that scare or worry them, and yet others chase to catch prey. Being chased by a dog is not pleasant and it can be dangerous for people and other animals, in addition to being potentially life-threatening for the dog. Teaching dogs to chase toys instead of people and other dogs gives them an acceptable alternative outlet for this natural behaviour.

The thrill of the chase

Dogs have descended from wolves that needed to chase and catch fast-moving prey. All dogs enjoy chasing, but in some breeds this trait has been accentuated. It is probably most enhanced in the herding breeds, which were bred to chase livestock, albeit in a controlled way, and in sight hounds, which were bred to look for game, then chase it.

Dogs that are kept as pets may not be given an outlet for this behaviour. If they have a strong genetic propensity for chasing, they will often find their own things to chase instead. They may chase joggers, cars, people on bicycles, livestock, other animals or their own tails. Such things often generate great excitement in dogs that are attracted to fast-moving objects, and, if they are able, they will give chase.

▲ Chasing other dogs in play is one way to use up the desire to chase. This drive is particularly strong in the herding breeds and hounds.

The predatory sequence

Track → watch → stalk → **chase** → bite → kill → dissect → eat
Herding dogs and sight hounds have been developed by breeding from those dogs with an enhanced enjoyment for the 'chase'.

▲ Chasing toys is a more acceptable outlet for chase energies as these games can then be controlled by the owner.

Preventing the behaviour

If possible, it is always best to prevent this from becoming a problem by teaching dogs to chase fast-moving toys in puppyhood. If a dog has already begun to chase inappropriate things, it is necessary to control this while encouraging him to play with toys instead, and teaching a chase recall for emergencies (see page 107). Once the dog is obsessed with playing with toys, he should be taught to ignore other things that he once chased and to chase his toys instead. Since most dogs, particularly those from herding breeds, usually like to chase toys, this is relatively easy to do. Hounds can be more problematic as they are often not as interested in toys as other dogs, and more work is needed to help them to realize how exciting chasing toys can be.

Chasing created by fear

Some dogs have learnt that the best way to get rid of something they see as a threat is to chase it away. If they are rewarded for this behaviour, they will learn to do it again. For example, a shy puppy is walked too close to fast moving traffic. The cars and lorries frighten him and the noise and movement make him excited enough to lunge and bark. He is rewarded by the traffic moving away and this encourages him to do it more. Later, when he is off the lead, he chases the traffic. Even if dogs are run over in pursuit of vehicles, they do not stop this activity as they still feel the need to chase these monsters away.

Cat chasing

Dogs chase cats for the same reasons that they chase other animals, either because they enjoy it, or they see them as prey, or because they are worried about them and want to get rid of them from their house and garden.

Taking on a new dog or cat can be a hazardous time, and care is needed by the owner until the dog learns to see the cat as part of his pack. Outside the house, fast-moving dogs such as Lurchers and Greyhounds need to wear muzzles and shoud be kept on lead in areas where cats may be. It is also necessary to take care in their own garden where they may catch a cat as it tries to get away. Going out first to 'shoo' any cats out of the garden may prevent a catastrophe.

▲ Restraining puppies so that they cannot chase cats will help to teach them to remain calm around them.

Chase aggression

Dogs may be aggressive when they catch up with the things that they are chasing for one of several reasons. They may bite through excitement, in frustration, to stop the thing moving, or often as a pre-emptive strike against something that hurt them the last time they chased it, such as a jogger who kicked out at them. They may also see the animal that they are chasing as prey and try to kill it.

If your dog has chased a person or an animal and has then been aggressive, it is important to get professional help in order to overcome the problem safely and successfully. You are legally and financially responsible for your dog's behaviour, and chase aggression is not well tolerated by society. Control in the form of muzzles, leads and only exercising in safe areas is needed until you can get help. Always use the open-box style of muzzle rather than the tube type so that air can circulate around the dog's mouth, which is very important for cooling a dog down after a run. Tube muzzles may look neater but they can lead to dogs collapsing if they get overheated.

▲ Teaching a dog how to play with toys will mean the owner is put back in control of the dog's desire to chase, preventing a situation where it may be aggressive to things it catches.

Questions and Answers

Q *My Lurcher Barney is two years old and has a lovely temperament. He is great with other dogs, adults and children, but his previous owner used to take him coursing and he will chase anything that moves, even cats. Is there any way of stopping him doing this?*

A Lurchers have been specially bred for hunting and so it is a natural and instinctive behaviour for them to chase and kill small animals. As well as a genetic makeup that makes him likely to want to do this, Barney's early life was spent developing and accentuating this trait.

Sadly, once the inherited desire is reinforced in this way, it becomes too ingrained for it to be eradicated, no matter how much training you try to do. For him, there is no difference between your neighbours' cats and the rabbits that he used to chase.

The best solution is to keep Barney on a lead whenever you are likely to encounter small animals and to keep him well away from other people's pets. When you do let him off, make sure he wears a muzzle so he cannot bite. Even with a muzzle on, impact with another animal can cause serious injuries, so only let him off when you are sure there are none around.

▲ Lurchers can run at speeds greater than most other animals and so are potentially lethal once they have decided that an animal is prey.

Q *I have had my seven-month-old Dalmatian, April, for four weeks. She will not let my three cats into our house. They will only come in if I block her off, and she chases them away if they are out in the garden. I have tried to hold the cats so she can sniff or lick them and I have put them in a room together for a long time hoping she will get used to them. None of this has worked. What can I do?*

A Being young and lively, April will seem quite terrifying to the cats and it is not surprising that they keep out of her way. However, the situation is not hopeless, and you will need to teach her how to behave when the cats are present. This will involve restraining her, not the cats.

Bring the cats in a meal times and make sure she is shut in another room for a while until they gain confidence about coming back in. Encourage the cats into the room where she is, but make sure she lies down quietly at the other end. It will be helpful to exercise her well beforehand so that she is tired and ready to lie down. Make her be still and quiet, tethering her so that she cannot get out of the 'down' position (make sure you teach her this slowly and gently beforehand so that she does not panic). Praise her if she is calm and ignore her when she is not.

Let her see you making a fuss of the cats and let them have the freedom of the house for while. When she has learned to be calm in their presence, which may take many sessions, allow her a bit more freedom but keep her under strict control and put her into the 'down' again if she gets excited. Progress in this way, both inside and outside the house, until she has learned to behave well around them.

Q We have recently moved into a house with our two-year-old Lurcher bitch. In the garden lives a cockerel. The dog is fascinated by the bird and walks after it, then gives chase. There is much clucking and squawking until the poor cockerel seeks refuge off the ground. To my knowledge, she's never actually got hold of the bird but she is absolutely focused on it and quivers and trembles in anticipation of chasing it. What can I do to stop this?

A To your Lurcher it is, at the moment, just a game. To the cockerel, it is a matter of life or death. Although your dog may not mean to hurt it, the inequality of size means that injuries for the bird are extremely likely. If it does not stop soon, your dog will get more skilled at the game or faster at giving chase and, eventually, the cockerel will be no more. Your dog needs to be taught how to behave with the cockerel. This is possible if she does not have a highly developed predatory instinct. It is unlikely that she does or, after a week of practising, she would have found a way to kill the cockerel. It is more likely that she just enjoys the sport of trying to catch it.

You are taking action once the behaviour has started or after it has finished; this is not effective because animals find it hard to learn from this. Instead, you need to do something before the behaviour begins. This means that, for a while, *all* visits to the garden must be supervised, unless you can erect a barrier to protect the bird. At first, keep your dog on a lead, keep her calm and don't let her walk fast in the cockerel's direction. Praise her when she relaxes, then take her away and repeat. It will take time but she will learn how to behave eventually. To speed this up, tether her where she can't harm the bird but can see it and not give chase (make sure the cockerel can't get to her either!). She must have plenty of activity and chase games with toys away from the bird to use up excess energy before you begin. Gradually, she will become bored with the cockerel's presence and will leave it alone.

◀ This cockerel has a safe haven away from the dog who is interested in it. Excited chase behaviour can quickly turn into predation, and a physical barrier is safer than trying to exert mental control to subdue the behaviour.

Chase recall

Teaching your dog to be recalled from a chase may save his life. This exercise requires dedication, time and patience.

Stage 1

■ You must stop all inappropriate chase games for your dog, and all games with other dogs for the time being.

■ Teach your dog to play with toys. Use soft toys at first, or hard toys filled with food, and try to get your dog to play at all moments of the day when he gets excited. Play little and often and always leave your dog wanting more. Have fun and make sure that you are both enjoying the games. Teach him to retrieve by having two toys. When he brings back the first one, tease him with the second toy, waiting until he has dropped the toy he was carrying before throwing the toy you are holding.

■ Begin in the house and garden, then on walks. This stage may take a long time, but you should see a steady improvement. Only go to the next stage when your dog is obsessed with toys and will chase them repeatedly on walks.

Stage 2

Once your dog is very keen to chase, you need to shout 'leave!' and prevent him from reaching the toy when it is thrown; twice out of every 10 throws at random. You can do this either by:

■ Having someone in front of you catch and hide the toy that you throw *or*

■ Waiting until your dog is some distance away, then throwing the toy so that he has to run past you in order to get it, stopping him with your voice as he approaches the toy, and then picking it up before he does if necessary.

As soon as the dog begins to slow up and leaves the toy he was chasing, then wave his favourite toy and call him, throwing the toy in the opposite direction to the first for him to chase. It may take several sessions for him to learn that 'leave' means that there is no point in continuing with his chase, and that you have something more interesting for him to chase instead.

Stage 3

Practise this until your dog is coming back to you for a game with the second toy as soon as he hears the word 'Leave!' Then set up a situation where you can practise a chase recall from whatever he usually chases. Practise at a distance, slowly getting closer to the thing that he likes to chase, and using a long line to prevent him running off in case your first attempts fail.

Eventually, your dog should learn that it is no longer rewarding for him to chase inappropriate things and that you can provide a very exciting game of chase that he can win instead. You must be patient; it may take time, but it will be worth the effort.

Questions and Answers

Q *We obtained an 18-month-old Husky from a rescue centre. With his previous owner, he once chased a herd of goats, even cornering one and inflicting some wounds on her rear which required extensive stitching by a vet. Is there any thing we can do to reform his behaviour?*

A There are two elements that contribute towards livestock attacks by dogs: the desire to chase, and the instinct to catch and to kill. Both of these require a predisposition that comes from their genes, and the resulting behaviour will need to be developed and honed by practice. Huskies have a rather primitive genetic makeup and their instincts to catch and kill prey are nearly as strong as those of their wolf ancestors. Unfortunately, once your dog has learned how much fun it is to do this, then stopping him is extremely unlikely.

If he were a dog that liked to play with toys, you could, with some hard work, teach him to relate better to you, to learn chase recalls and have him under enough control to stop the chase before it started. Unfortunately, however, Huskies are not 'object players' and therefore usually they cannot be trained to be obsessive about toys in the same way.

Really, your best solution is to keep him leashed unless you can give him freedom in an enclosed area. Since Huskies really require several miles' walking a day if they are to be reasonably contented, you will have to make a decision about whether or not this is possible given your circumstances.

▶ Huskies have been bred to be efficient long-distance runners and their predatory instincts are very strong.

CASE HISTORY

A TV addict

Dog: Skye, West Highland White Terrier, seven years, neutered male

Background

Skye's elderly owner took him to the veterinary surgeon one day to be put to sleep. Skye was an active healthy little dog but her owner was at the end of her tether. She was unable to spend evenings quietly sitting watching television as Skye would bark and jump at the moving images on the screen. She was also tormented during the day by frantic barking whenever she walked past the set, even when it was switched off. Skye had become so addicted to barking that the owner could no longer cope with the situation. She was also worried about the noise disturbing her elderly neighbours.

The problem had begun three years before when they had moved into a new flat. The television set was down at Skye's level and he enjoyed watching wildlife and animal programmes. His owner had encouraged this and had begun to put certain programmes on especially for him because she knew he enjoyed them. Gradually, the enjoyment became an obsession and his life began to revolve around chasing anything that moved on the screen.

This was a real problem during the winter months when Skye's exercise was restricted. His owner, being elderly, was concerned about falling over in the mud, and there was a lack of clean places around her home where she could walk him. As well as restricted exercise, the opportunities to play games with toys were reduced because he was spending so much time watching television. The games he was playing with the TV were less satisfying than real games so he had to play more often and more persistently.

Skye's owner loved him, having raised him from a puppy, and he was her only constant source of companionship. However, living with him was making her ill. She could not entertain the idea of him going into rescue and being rehomed to someone she did not know, so she decided that a one-way trip to the veterinary surgery was the only option open to her in the circumstances. Luckily, however, the veterinary surgeon advised her to consult a pet behaviour counselor and a consultation was arranged for the following day.

Observations and diagnosis

Skye was an active, energetic dog and the flat was small without a garden. His life has become very restricted when his male owner had died and the female owner had to leave their house with a garden and move into the small flat. Since Skye was an adult dog by this time, his owner had thrown away most of his toys thinking that he would not need them as he was not a puppy any more. More buildings were being constructed around the block of flats where they lived and most of the areas that should have been grass were mud. Skye's owner kept the flat neat and tidy, and a dog that was covered in mud would cause considerable mess.

The only exciting things in life for Skye were the television and his owner. He was not getting enough exercise or play and had taken to chasing things on TV as a way to use up all his energies. This unacceptable behaviour had become a bad habit. The relationship with his owner had deteriorated recently as she had become increasingly desperate about his behaviour. As she had withdrawn from him, Skye found that the only way to get attention was to bark incessantly, causing her to shout at him. This was better than no attention at all, and the attention-seeking barking had added to the problem of him barking when he was chasing objects on television.

Treatment plan

We asked a neighbour who had his own dog which he took for long walks everyday if he would take Skye with them and he agreed. We trained Skye to stand still in the sink to be washed and to sit quietly on a mat to be dried. When he came home from his walks, he was picked up in an old towel on the doorstep and then taken to the sink to be washed so that the minimum disruption was caused to the flat. A variety of new squeaky toys was bought for Skye, and a new play and attention regime was instigated, with him playing his favourite game of chasing squeaky toys and being given attention little and often throughout the day. Although the flat was small, there was a long stretch of carpet from the kitchen to the front door. Skye's owner could use this to give him a good long chase, and when he brought the toy back, yet another and another.

Once these routines were put into place, Skye's addiction to the television was broken by asking the owner to go without television for one week. When she started to watch again, she tied Skye down next to her chair so that he could not see the screen without standing up. Since he was a long way from the screen, he was prevented from chasing the images. The set was raised onto a small table so that, during the day, he was not encouraged to think about images moving on the screen. Periods of good behaviour with no barking were rewarded by exciting games with toys.

Outcome

After a few days, the new routine gave Skye a more fulfilling outlet for his energies and he began to stop barking at his owner for attention. When the TV was turned on again, he started to bark again for a short time, but quickly gave up once he realized he could not get to it. Eventually his addiction was broken altogether and he lived a much more satisfying and fulfilled life.

Questions and Answers

Q *Can you settle an argument? My wife says it's wrong to hit the dog for being naughty. But I will still slap our children if they are doing something dangerous like playing with electric plugs and it certainly stops them so why shouldn't we hit the dog if we catch him stealing or chewing something? I think we've all gone too soft but my wife says she'll thump me if I so much as raise a hand to our dog!*

A Humans are quite aggressive as a species and it is natural to lash out when we are frightened or frustrated. Children and animals usually get hit for these reasons rather than as part of a calculated discipline intended to make them behave better. It has been proven in scientific experiments that punishment is an ineffective way of helping animals to learn, particularly if it happens after the behaviour started or, worse, after it has finished. A nasty experience that occurs when the behaviour begins and ends when it stops is effective, but this is difficult to get right in practice. People often go way over the top, resulting in the animal becoming frightened. And frightened animals are thinking more about survival than they are about learning how to behave.

Punishment spoils the relationship we have with our pets, making them mistrustful of people. Dogs that are punished a lot learn to bite rather than learning a different way to deal with problems. Owners who don't punish usually have such a good relationship with their pets that they respond well to a little scolding. You need boundaries that your dog will not cross; this can be done with peaceful means.

So what do we do instead? Well, dogs are creatures of habit and once good habits are in place and are being rewarded, they are less likely to behave badly. Think ahead and prevent bad behaviour; reward the good behaviour when it happens. If your dog wants to jump up to greet you, prevent him by holding his collar or turning your back until he has calmed down, and then reward the good behaviour by getting down to his level and making a big fuss of him.

It is also important to ensure all of your dog's species needs are met: he has things to chew other than the carpet; he gets enough exercise and mental stimulation. A contented dog is usually a well-behaved dog so rather than shouting or hitting, think about why he is mis-behaving and teach him to behave better or attend to his species needs instead.

Chapter 8

Car travel problems

Car travel problems are common among dogs. Many are a result of an imperfect introduction to car travel at an early age or due to frights, such as those caused by an accident in later life. Others may be due to existing behaviour problems that are accentuated by close confinement inside a car. Finding a solution relies on looking for the reason that the dog is showing unwanted behaviour and solving the problem for the dog.

Fear of car travel

Many dogs are worried about being in a car. Inside the car, they do not have a seat to sit in that keeps them held comfortably. As a result, they are often thrown around by the movement of the car as it lurches, twists and turns.

Sitting on a shelf that moves up and down and also from side to side, particularly if you are too small to see where you are going, can be very frightening for a dog. Since most puppies are separated from their mothers just before their first car journey and are then taken to the vet for vaccinations after a ride in the car, this can add to their sense of fear which is associated with car travel.

Symptoms

Dogs that are afraid of car travel may be reluctant to get into a car. They may bark or chew at the upholstery to try to alleviate their feelings or may drool and be sick. These symptoms will begin as soon as the car is in motion. They may get worse when the car takes more turns, bumps and corners, and then get better on long straight roads, such as motorways.

▶ Sitting on a seat made for humans can mean that dogs are thrown around in the car much more than people. Many dogs learn to resist and corner as the car brakes and turns, but others become scared and show unwanted behaviour to try to deal with their feelings of fear.

Solutions

A gradual reintroduction to car travel is needed. Over many sessions, the dog needs to learn to be happy about getting into the car, having the doors closed and the engine started, moving slowly, then faster and taking corners until he can cope with normal driving. This may take a long time but it will be worth it in the long run. Make sure that your dog is enjoying each part of the process, and never go faster than he can cope with. Reward him with games and food when he stays calm so that good associations with the car develop.

Fear of things outside

Dogs may also bark to try to keep things away from the car that frighten them, such as other dogs, people or traffic. If your dog threatens and lunges from within the car, it is necessary to desensitize him to these things away from the car (see page 12). When he no longer perceives these things as a threat, he will cease to bark at them from within the car.

Questions and Answers

Q *Many good walks suitable for a Spaniel are a short car journey away (five to ten minutes). Our 15-week-old Spaniel, Rory, hates the car. We have to lift him in, and then, after a couple of minutes of the journey, he begins to salivate and is often sick. How can we avoid this?*

A Many puppies are worried about being in the car and their anxiety makes them drool and be sick. The best way for you to tackle this problem is to gradually desensitize your dog, taking things at his speed. More patience now will pay off in the long run. Begin by feeding him close to the car and playing with him with toys around it. Over several sessions, encourage him to move closer to the car and even jump inside for treats and games. Sit in the car with him and make it a pleasant experience.

When he can cope and is happy, close the doors. During later sessions, drive a few hundred metres, let him out and play or feed him. Put him back in, drive home and repeat. Gradually, over many weeks,

▲ Owning a dog that will travel easily in the car allows you to take him anywhere, and it is really worthwhile to spend time during his puppyhood to teach him to be unafraid of car travel.

increase the distance that he travels, never going further than he can cope with before he begins to show signs of unease. You should gradually begin to see an improvement and then you will progress faster. You should keep a diary to monitor your progress and stay motivated. Eventually, you will have a dog you can take anywhere by car.

Q *Our West Highland White Terrier, Sid, is terrible in the car. He whines and screams while pacing up and down on the back seat. After five or ten minutes of this noise and pacing, we get cross with him. He gets worse if we drive faster but seems to be a little better on long journeys. However, we mostly take him only on short journeys and nothing seems to calm him down. Would a car safety harness stop him?*

A Car safety harnesses are a very good idea to stop him flying through the windscreen, injuring you in the process during an accident, but they are unlikely to solve the problem. From what you say, it sounds as though Sid is frightened of being in the car and making a noise is his way of dealing with the anxiety he feels. Getting cross with him will only serve to increase his anxieties and it doesn't work anyway. If he is afraid, the only way to help him is to get him used to car travel gradually. Take it slowly, at his speed, and give him lots of short, slow, happy rides that end in a fun walk, a game with toys or anything else he enjoys. As he begins to learn that car travel is safe, the trips can be gradually faster and longer.

▶ A dog loose in the car can become a dangerous projectile during an accident. To prevent injury to both the dog and others, attach him to the seat with a car harness.

Other common problems

There are many causes for dogs experiencing travel problems and some of the most common ones are listed below.

Excitement in the car

Many dogs are taken by car to the place where they will be walked. This can make them very excited whenever they are in the car as they cannot wait to get out. Some may jump around excitedly and bark, usually in a high-pitched screaming manner, keeping it up until the car stops, whereas others may bite at the upholstery or even at other dogs or people in the car in their frustration at not being able to get there fast enough.

These dogs need to learn to deal with the frustration they feel at not being able to get what they want (see page 76). Initially, it is easiest to do this outside of the car. They also need to learn that riding in the car no longer ends in high excitement. This means that they need to be taken on many journeys where they only get out when the owner returns home. When you get to the park, or the place where you will be walking your dog, take a book and read until your dog is quiet. Only let him out of the car when he is quiet and, before you let him off, do some quiet obedience exercises with him to change his expectations of his arrival at that place. It will also help if he is tired before being put into the car so a vigorous game in the garden beforehand can help take the edge off his energy.

Attention-seeking in the car

Another reason why dogs bark in the car is to attract our attention. Such dogs are often controlling in their home environment and have usually found ways to get their owner's undivided attention whenever they want it. In the car, the owner's attention is on the road ahead, particularly if driving, and their dog is confined at the back of a car behind a dog guard. These dogs often bark continuously, with a regular-paced bark, while staring at the back of their owner's head. They usually continue in this vein until their owner stops the car and pays some attention to them.

To solve this problem, it is more comfortable to get the dog used to being ignored in a home environment. Once the dog is accustomed to being ignored at home (see page 31), the same treatment can be applied to car travel.

Chase motivated problems

Some dogs that enjoy chasing moving objects often get very excited when they are in the car. Things go past the windows at high speed, and it is great fun to try to chase them. Dogs that engage in this sort of behaviour will often fix on a certain object, such as a telegraph pole or perhaps another dog, barking excitedly as it gets closer and hopping from foot to foot in their excitement. As the object goes past, they will spin round trying to follow it, barking furiously, and then begin looking for the next thing to chase. If they are left unrestrained, some dogs will rush from seat to seat or will bite the upholstery in their frustration at not being able to give chase properly.

A quick solution is to confine these dogs in a place inside the car from which they cannot see things approaching – an ideal place would be an indoor kennel or a cage with a cover over it. Alternatively, you could secure them in one of the foot wells using a car harness so that they cannot see out of the windows.

For a longer-term solution, teach them how to retrieve a toy and then play with them frequently throughout the day to give them an outlet for their desire to chase things. Later, you can teach them to deal with the frustration of not being able to chase when they want to (see page 76) and then re-teach this in the car, preventing any unwanted behaviour and rewarding quiet, calm behaviour.

Destructiveness in the car when left alone

Some dogs may be destructive when they are left alone in the car for all the reasons that are given in Chapter 2, such as fear of isolation or boredom. Dogs that are insecure and feel the need to surround themselves with material that smells of their owner will often chew things that carry their scent, such as seat belts, the steering wheel, gear stick and seats. Since these objects are expensive, the owner often thinks erroneously that the dog has acted out of spite. To solve this problem, turn back to Chapter 2.

Car guarding

The car is a small space, which is easily defended, and fearful dogs often prefer to be inside such places. This may result in them lunging out at people or dogs that happen to be passing by if the tailgate or door is left open. Always take care with such dogs when they are in the car (see Chapters 1 and 4 for solutions).

Questions and Answers

Q *My three dogs used to be so well behaved but they are becoming more naughty every day. They have started barking whenever they get their leads on and in the car as we approach their favourite walk. They also bark as we turn into our road on the way home and all the way into the house. I have trained the one that started it to bark on command but once they're all woofing and wagging there's no reasoning with them! Just as I get one quiet, then another starts woofing. Please can you advise what I should do about this?*

A Excited barking is quite infectious and it appears that the other two dogs have caught on and are now joining in. Any behaviour that is rewarded will happen more often, so any attention from you, even if you are scolding them, will add to the reward that they are getting from barking and will make the problem even worse. It may even seem to them as though you are joining in, so do not tell them to stop or shout at them when they are barking; instead, you should use clever tactics to stop them.

Barking is fuelled by excitement so once it has started you must ensure that your dogs are not rewarded by further movement and fun.

▲ A dog's excitement at the thought of an imminent walk is increased if there are other dogs to go for a run with.

▲ Jumping out of the car with friends often causes great excitement, and it may be better to take one dog out slowly on a lead at a time.

For example, when you are putting on their leads, stop and stand still if any of your dogs begins to bark. Don't say anything at all and just stay calm. Eventually, the excitement will dissolve and the dogs will become quiet, thereby allowing you to reward them by getting on with the process of taking them out.

Continue with this process, stopping and starting as necessary, until you have got them all out of the house quietly and back in again. It may take a long time at first, but, eventually, they will realize that they do not go anywhere fast when they are making a noise and will learn to be quiet.

The barking in the car will be due to the excitement caused by anticipation of what will happen when the car stops. Jumping out with your friends is lots of fun, and they are all excited at the prospect. To stop this, do not get out as soon as you turn off the engine. Put in ear plugs and read a good book until they are all quiet and settled. When they get out, make them walk quietly in the same way as you did when you left the house for at least five minutes. In this way, you will reduce their expectation of fun at the end of the journey which should result in a more peaceful ride in the car.

CASE HISTORY

Barking in the car

Dog: Sam, black Labrador cross, nine years, neutered male

Background

Sam was a rescue dog, who was obtained by his present owners at one year old. He had been terrified of men but his owners had overcome that problem and now he was quite confident with male strangers. However, his problem was in the car where he would bark continuously. He always jumped in eagerly but, once the engine was switched on, he would not stop barking. The owners enjoyed taking him away for weekends but they found journeys with him were exhausting. The only time that he was quiet was after a long stretch of motorway driving during which he

lay down and went to sleep. However, as soon as they turned off the motorway or braked, Sam would be up at once and the barking would start all over again. The owners found themselves not talking on long journeys in case Sam woke up and started barking.

Observations and diagnosis

A car journey with Sam soon revealed that his problem was fear of the movement of the car. He enjoyed sitting in a stationary vehicle, even jumping in by himself if the door was left open. When the engine was turned on, however, he started to bark but became quiet again if the car remained stationary. Sam's barking began in earnest when the car started to move forward. He then gave a fast, high-pitched repetitive bark, which was indicative of anxiety. He did not move about in the car but sat still, looking worried and taking no notice of his owners, no matter how much they tried to comfort him.

The owners were then asked to drive faster around corners and over bumps, and this caused Sam to increase his rate of barking slightly. As the speed of the car picked up, he drooled saliva and looked increasingly unhappy. However, when the car slowed down, his rate of barking also slowed down.

Treatment plan

Sam had never really learnt to cope with travelling in a car so a slow, gradual reintroduction programme was advised. This involved short, slow journeys at first which always ended in fun, games and a reward. To begin with, it was enough just to go just to the end of the drive, then stop and take him out for a walk or feed him his dinner, or play with some toys. His barking was used to monitor his anxiety, and the owners were advised to proceed at a pace that did not cause him to bark. If he barked, then they had to slow down. The owners were also asked not to reassure him when he barked as this could confirm his fear and make him even worse.

Outcome

The owners stuck rigidly to the treatment plan and Sam soon learned not to be afraid in the car. They took things slowly and gradually so that Sam learned that not only was he safe but that a ride in the car always ended in something nice happening, such as a walk or a game. Gradually he became more confident in the car and eventually the owners were able to take him on holiday in peace.

Useful information

Association of Pet Behaviour Counsellors
PO Box 46
Worcester WR8 9YS
www.apbc.org.uk

Puppy School
PO Box 186
Chipping Norton
Oxon OX7 3XG
www.puppyschool.co.uk

Acknowledgements
The author is very grateful to More Th>n and to *Dogs Today* for allowing her to reproduce the questions and answers that previously appeared on the 'Ask the Experts' section of the www.pethealthcare.co.uk website and in the 'Ask the panel ...' section of the *Dogs Today* magazine.

Further help
Training classes will help you to learn the skills and techniques needed to train effectively, and provide help and encouragement. Classes vary in quality so select carefully from those available. Only go to those that use reward-based methods in a friendly, easy-to-learn environment. Avoid those where check chains or force is used and where the mood is humiliating or chaotic.

If your dog has a behaviour problem, you will need to find someone who has an in-depth understanding of dog behaviour. They need to have been working with dogs for many years to gain the necessary experience, so check their work history carefully. A recommendation from someone who has tried out their methods or a referral from a vet is often the best way to find the right person. Also, they should be using only effective, humane methods so avoid anyone who offers quick fixes in the form of aversion or punishment.

Index

If you have enjoyed this book, why not learn more about 'man's best friend' with other Collins titles?

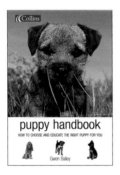

Expert advice to enable you to choose and train a friendly and sociable puppy, using gentle and effective methods

128pp   £7.99
PB   0 00 714264 1

An essential handbook with clear step-by-step photography which makes training your dog simple and enjoyable

128pp   £7.99
PB   0 00 714256 0

The Collins Dog Owner's Guide series includes:

Boxer
PB   0 00 413370 6

Cocker Spaniel
PB   0 00 717607 4

English Springer Spaniel
PB   0 00 717605 8

German Shepherd
PB   0 00 717833 6

Labrador
PB   0 00 717832 8

West Highland White Terrier
PB   0 00 717831 X

Yorkshire Terrier
PB   0 00 717606 6

144pp   £7.99

To order any of these titles, please telephone **0870 787 1732**
For further information about all Collins books, visit our website: **www.collins.co.uk**

BIBLIO RPL Ltée

G — JUIL. 2005